Bloom's
GUIDES

Tennessee Williams's
A Streetcar Named Desire

1984
The Adventures of Huckleberry Finn
All the Pretty Horses
Beloved
Brave New World
The Chosen
The Crucible
Cry, the Beloved Country
Death of a Salesman
The Grapes of Wrath
Great Expectations
Hamlet
The Handmaid's Tale
The House on Mango Street
I Know Why the Caged Bird Sings
The Iliad
Lord of the Flies
Macbeth
Maggie: A Girl of the Streets
The Member of the Wedding
Pride and Prejudice
Ragtime
Romeo and Juliet
The Scarlet Letter
Snow Falling on Cedars
A Streetcar Named Desire
The Things They Carried
To Kill a Mockingbird

Bloom's
GUIDES

Tennessee Williams's
A Streetcar Named Desire

Edited & with an Introduction
by Harold Bloom

CHELSEA HOUSE
P U B L I S H E R S
A Haights Cross Communications Company ®

Philadelphia

© 2005 by Chelsea House Publishers, a subsidiary of Haights Cross Communications.

A Haights Cross Communications ⬩ Company ®

www.chelseahouse.com

Contributing editor: Camille-Yvette Welsch
Cover design by Takeshi Takahashi
Layout by EJB Publishing Services

Introduction © 2005 by Harold Bloom.

Printed and bound in the United States of America.

First Printing
1 3 5 7 9 8 6 4 2

Library of Congress Cataloging-in-Publication Data
Tennessee Williams's A streetcar named Desire / [edited and with an introduction by] Harold Bloom.
    p. cm. — (Bloom's guides)
  Includes bibliographical references.
  ISBN 0-7910-8242-3 (alk. paper)
  1. Williams, Tennessee, 1911-1983. Streetcar named Desire. 2. New Orleans (La.)—In literature. I. Title: Streetcar named Desire. II. Bloom, Harold. III. Series.
  PS3545.I5365S837 2005
  812'.54—dc22
                              2004030477

Contents

Introduction

HAROLD BLOOM

It is a sad and inexplicable truth that the United States, a dramatic nation, continues to have so limited a literary achievement in the drama. American literature, from Emerson to the present moment, is a distinguished tradition. The poetry of Whitman, Dickinson, Frost, Stevens, Eliot, W.C. Williams, Hart Crane, R.P. Warren, Elizabeth Bishop down through the generation of my own contemporaries—John Ashbery, James Merrill, A.R. Ammons, and others—has an unquestionable eminence, and takes a vital place in Western literature. Prose fiction from Hawthorne and Melville on through Mark Twain and Henry James to Cather and Dreiser, Faulkner, Hemingway, Fitzgerald, Nathanael West, and Pynchon, has almost a parallel importance. The line of essayists and critics from Emerson and Thoreau to Kenneth Burke and beyond constitutes another crucial strand of our national letters. But where is the American drama in comparison to all this, and in relation to the long cavalcade of western drama from Aeschylus to Beckett?

The American theater, by the common estimate of its most eminent critics, touches an initial strength with Eugene O'Neill, and then proceeds to the more varied excellences of Thornton Wilder, Tennessee Williams, Arthur Miller, Edward Albee, and Sam Shepard. That sequence is clearly problematical, and becomes even more worrisome when we move from playwrights to plays. Which are our dramatic works that matter most? *Long Day's Journey Into Night*, certainly; perhaps *The Iceman Cometh*; evidently *A Streetcar Named Desire* and *Death of a Salesman*; perhaps again *The Skin of Our Teeth* and *The Zoo Story*—it is not God's plenty. And I will venture the speculation that our drama palpably is not yet literary enough. By this I do not just mean that O'Neill writes very badly, or Miller very baldly; they do, but so did Dreiser, and *Sister Carrie* and *An American Tragedy* prevail nevertheless. Nor do I wish to be an American Matthew Arnold (whom I loathe above all other critics) and proclaim that our dramatists simply have not known enough. They know more than enough, and that is part of the trouble.

Literary tradition, as I have come to understand it, masks the agon between past and present as a benign relationship, whether personal or societal. The actual transferences between the force of the literary past and the potential of writing in the present tend to be darker, even if they do not always or altogether follow the defensive patterns of what Sigmund Freud called "family romances." Whether or not ambivalence, however repressed, towards the past's force is felt by the new writer and is manifested in his work seems to depend entirely upon the ambition and power of the oncoming artist. If he aspires after strength, and can attain it, then he must struggle with both a positive and a negative transference, false connections become necessarily imagined ones, between a composite precursor and himself. His principal resource in that agon will be his own native gift for interpretation, or as I am inclined to call it, strong misreading. Revising his precursor, he will create himself, make himself into a kind of changeling, and so he will become, in an illusory but highly pragmatic way, his own father.

The most literary of our major dramatists, and clearly I mean "literary" in a precisely descriptive sense, neither pejorative nor eulogistic, was Tennessee Williams. Wilder, with his intimate connections to *Finnegan's Wake* and Gertrude Stein, might seem to dispute this placement, and Wilder was certainly more literate than Williams. But Wilder had a benign relation to his crucial precursor, Joyce, and did not aspire after a destructive strength. Williams did, and suffered the fate he prophesied and desired; the strength destroyed his later work, and his later life, and thus joined itself to the American tradition of self-destructive genius. Williams truly had one precursor only: Hart Crane, the greatest of our lyrical poets, after Whitman and Dickinson, and the most self-destructive figure in our national literature, surpassing all others in this, as in so many regards.

Williams asserted he had other precursors also: D.H. Lawrence, and Chekhov in the drama. These were outward influences, and benefited Williams well enough, but they were essentially formal, and so not the personal and societal family romance of authentic poetic influence. Hart Crane made Williams into more of a dramatic lyrist, though writing in prose, than the lyrical dramatist that Williams is supposed to have been. Though this influence—perhaps more nearly an identification—helped form *The Glass Menagerie* and (less overtly) *A Streetcar Named Desire*, and in a lesser mode *Summer and Smoke* and *Suddenly Last Summer*, it also led to such disasters of misplaced lyricism as the dreadful *Camino Real* and the dreary *The Night of the Iguana*. (*Cat on a Hot Tin Roof*, one of Williams's best plays, does not seem to me to show any influence of Crane.) Williams's long aesthetic decline covered thirty years, from 1953 to 1983, and reflected the sorrows of a seer who, by his early forties, had outlived his own vision. Hart Crane, self-slain at thirty-two, had set for Williams a High Romantic paradigm that helped cause Williams, his heart as dry as summer dust, to burn to the socket.

II

The epigraph to *A Streetcar Named Desire* is a quatrain from Hart Crane's "The Broken Tower," the poet's elegy for his gift, his vocation, his life, and so Crane's precise equivalent of Shelley's *Triumph of Life*, Keat's *Fall of Hyperion*, and Whitman's "When Lilacs Last in the Dooryard Bloom'd." Tennessee Williams, in his long thirty years of decline after composing *A Streetcar Named Desire*, had no highly designed, powerfully executed elegy for his own poetic self. Unlike Crane, his American Romantic precursor and aesthetic paradigm, Williams had to live out the slow degradation of the waning of his potential, and so endured the triumph of life over his imagination.

Streetcar sustains a first rereading, after thirty years away from it, more strongly than I had expected. It is, inevitably, more remarkable on the stage than in the study, but the fusion of Williams's lyrical and dramatic talents in it has prevailed over time, at least so far. The play's flaws, in performance, ensue from its implicit tendency to sensationalize its characters, Blanche DuBois in particular. Directors and actresses have made such sensationalizing altogether explicit, with the sad result prophesied by Kenneth Tynan many years ago. The playgoer forgets that Blanche's only strengths are "nostalgia and home," that she is "the desperate exceptional woman," and that her fall is a parable, rather than an isolated squalor:

When, finally, she is removed to the mental home, we should feel that a part of civilization is going with her. Where ancient drama teaches us to reach nobility by contemplation of what is noble, modern American drama conjures us to contemplate what might have been noble, but is now humiliated, ignoble in the sigh of all but the compassionate.

Tynan, though accurate enough, still might have modified the image of Blanche taking a part of civilization away with her into madness. Though Blanche yearns for the values of the aesthetic, she scarcely embodies them, being in this failure a masochistic self-parody on the part of Williams himself. His *Memoirs* portray Williams incessantly in the role of Blanche, studying the nostalgias, and inching along the wavering line between hope and paranoia. Williams, rather than Blanche, sustains Tynan's analysis of the lost nobility, now humiliated, that American drama conjures us to contemplate.

The fall of Blanche is a parable, not of American civilization's lost nobility, but of the failure of the American literary imagination to rise above its recent myths of recurrent defeat. Emerson admonished us, his descendants, to go beyond the Great Defeat of the Crucifixion and to demand Victory instead, a victory of the senses as well as of the soul. Walt Whitman, taking up Emerson's challenge directly, set the heroic pattern so desperately emulated by Hart Crane, and which is then repeated in a coarser tone in Williams's life and work.

It must seem curious, at first, to regard Blanche DuBois as a failed Whitmanian, but essentially that is her aesthetic identity. Confronted by the revelation of her young husband's preference for an older man over herself, Blanche falls downwards and outwards into nymphomania, phantasmagoric hopes, pseudo-imaginative collages of memory and desire. Her Orphic, psychic rending by the amiably brutal Stanley Kowalski, a rough but effective version of D.H. Lawrence's vitalistic vision of male force, is pathetic rather than tragic, not because Stanley necessarily is mindless, but because she unnecessarily has made herself mindless, by failing the pragmatic test of experience.

Williams's most effective blend of lyrical vision and dramatic irony in the play comes in the agony of Blanche's cry against Stanley to Stella, his wife and her sister:

He acts like an animal, has an animal's habits! Eats like one, moves like one, talks like one! There's even something—subhuman—something not quite to the stage of humanity yet! Yes, something—ape-like about him, like one of those pictures I've seen in—anthropological studies! Thousands and thousands of years have passed him right by, and there he is—Stanley Kowalski—survivor of the stone age! Bearing the raw meat home from the kill in the jungle! And you—*you* here—*waiting* for him! Maybe he'll strike you or maybe grunt and kiss you! That is, if kisses have been discovered yet! Night falls and the other apes gather! There in the front of the cave, all grunting like him, and swilling and gnawing and hulking! His poker night!—you call it—this party of apes! Somebody growls—some creature snatches at something—the fight is on! *God*! Maybe we are a long way from being made in God's image, but Stella—my sister—there has been *some* progress since then! Such things as art—as poetry and music—such kinds of new light have come into the world since then! IN some kinds of people some tenderer feelings have had some little beginning! That we have got to make *grow*! And *cling* to, and hold as our flag! In this dark march toward whatever it is we're approaching.... *Don't—don't hang back with the brutes!*

The lyricism here takes its strength from the ambivalence of what at once attracts and dismays both Blanche and Williams. Dramatic irony, terrible in its antithetic pathos, results here from Blanche's involuntary self-condemnation, since she herself has hung back with the brutes while merely blinking at the new light of the aesthetic. Stanley, being what he is, is clearly less to blame than Blanche, who was capable of more but failed in will.

Williams, in his *Memoirs*, haunted as always by Hart Crane, refers to his precursor as "a tremendous and yet fragile artist," and then associates both himself and Blanche with the fate of Crane, a suicide by drowning in the Caribbean:

I am as much of an hysteric as ... Blanche; a codicil to my will provides for the disposition of my body in this way. "Sewn up in a clean white sack and dropped over board, twelve hours north of Havana, so that my bones may rest not too far from those of Hart Crane ... "

At the conclusion of *Memoirs*, Williams again associated Crane both with his own vocation and his own limitations, following Crane even in an identification with the young Rimbaud:

A poet such as the young Rimbaud is the only writer of whom I can think, at this moment, who could escape from words into the sensations of being, through his youth, turbulent with revolution, permitted articulation by nights of absinthe. And of course there is Hart Crane. Both of these poets touched fire that burned them alive. And perhaps it is only through self-immolation of such a nature that we living beings can offer to you the entire truth of ourselves within the reasonable boundaries of a book.

It is the limitation of *Memoirs*, and in some sense even of *A Streetcar Named Desire*, that we cannot accept either Williams or poor Blanche as a Rimbaud or a Hart Crane. Blanche cannot be said to have touched fire that burned her alive. Yet Williams earns the relevance of the play's great epigraph to Blanche's terrible fate:

And so it was I entered the broken world
To trace the visionary company of love, its voice
An instant in the wind (I know not whither hurled)
But not for long to hold each desperate choice.

Biographical Sketch

Born in Columbus, Mississippi in 1911, Thomas Lanier Williams spent the first seven years of his childhood in the welcoming arms of his maternal grandparents Dakin, his sister, Rose, and his mother. His father, Cornelius, an overbearing and charismatic man, was often away on sales trips, leaving his son to slowly absorb southern mores and a nostalgia for the old South and its particular modes of articulation. The family moved to St. Louis, Missouri, when Williams was seven, where he and his sister, with their southern patrician manners, were taunted mercilessly, particularly the somewhat effeminate Williams, who had been coddled as a child after a prolonged and serious illness. Plagued, he grew even closer to his sister and began his lifelong process of writing stories and poems as escape from the ridicule of his peers and his father who took to calling his son, "Miss Nancy."

Williams's writing appeared in print for the first time when he was sixteen. His piece, "Can a Good Wife Be a Good Sport?" won an essay contest offered through *Smart Set* magazine. In 1929, he attended the University of Missouri only to be brought home by his father after failing his ROTC class in his junior year. His father secured him a job at the shoe factory in which he worked until Williams suffered a breakdown in 1935 whereupon he retired to his Dakin grandparents to recover. While in Memphis, he produced his first play, *Cairo, Shanghai, Bombay!* With the moral and financial support of his grandparents, Williams returned to college, this time at the University of Washington, although he quickly moved on to the University of Iowa where he immersed himself in the study of drama. While he was away at school, his mother responded to his sister Rose's increasing psychiatric problems by ordering a prefrontal lobotomy to be performed, leaving Rose with the intellect and outlook of a child for the rest of her long life. Though guilt-ridden over his inability to protect his sister, Williams received a BA in English in 1938.

It was 1939 that proved to be a provident year for Williams's budding career. He published in *Story* magazine and later that same year after craftily lying about his age and calling himself Tennessee, he won a Group Theater Prize of $100 which he used travel, visiting New Orleans, California, Mexico, and New Mexico. His plays caught the eye of New York agent, Audrey Wood, who took him on as a client, and then secured him a Rockefeller Foundation Grant which Williams used to write *Battle of Angels*. By 1940, he had moved to New York City, enrolling himself in an advanced playwriting class at The New School. With that training, he took odd jobs all over the country, living hand to mouth and working on the play that became *The Glass Menagerie* during his brief tenure as a script writer for MGM. He tried to pitch them the idea but was firmly refused. Two years later, the play that the studios had refused opened in Chicago on December 26. Initially the theater going public was apathetic; however, two theater critics scolded the public into attending and the drama quickly became a sensation, making its way to New York City where it premiered in 1945. It won the New York Critics Circle Award, the first of three for the playwright. The success terrified and silenced Williams for a brief time before he actively sought refuge from his new fame. Having fully acknowledged his own homosexuality, he fled to Provincetown, Massachusetts, a safe haven for homosexuals, and eventually, Key West and Mexico. In those places, he felt that he could return to the hard living that had made his playwriting rich and tense.

Williams followed *The Glass Menagerie* with perhaps his most famous play, *A Streetcar Named Desire*, which premiered in New York City. The play won the New York Critics Circle Award as well as the Pulitzer Prize. The next fifteen years were highly productive for Williams. He wrote and premiered a number of plays, *Summer and Smoke*, *The Rose Tattoo*, *The Camino Real*, *Cat on a Hot Tin Roof* (which received the Pulitzer and the New York Critics Circle Award), *Orpheus Descending*, an early version of *Something Unspoken* and *Suddenly Last Summer*, and *Sweet Bird of Youth*. In the meantime, the silver screen was making stars out of actors in Williams's plays. Marlon Brando became an overnight sensation, Geraldine Page cemented her place as a serious actress, and Karl Malden, Kim Hunter, and Vivien Leigh all won Oscars for their performances in *A Streetcar Named Desire*.

While living in New Orleans in 1947, Williams met the love of his life, Frank Merlo, with whom he had a relationship for almost sixteen years, breaking up shortly before Merlo's death. After the death of Merlo, Williams, unable to piece his life together without his balanced partner, turned more deeply to alcohol and drugs. Much of the sixties blurred into one long binge. Williams began every morning by smoking, guzzling coffee, and steadily pounding on his typewriter, abruptly changing fonts when a ribbon would wear out. In 1969, Williams's brother, Dakin, helped him to convert to Roman Catholicism and then had Williams committed, believing that his brother meant to kill himself. Williams remained in the psychiatric ward of a St. Louis hospital for three months. The experience left a permanent rift between the brothers. For his sister, Rose, however, Williams felt an undying affection. He took her out on the town, paid for her to have the best care, and fawned over her for the entirety of his life. Williams also remained quite close to his grandparents. After the death of his grandmother, Grandfather Dakin came to Key West to live with Williams and Merlo.

The 1960s also presented a change in the critical response to Williams. As his plays grew increasingly expressionistic, critics grew increasingly impatient, claiming that he had burned himself out, that his early brilliance was gone. The disparaging remarks in the newspapers cut deeply, and Williams found himself growing increasingly cynical and paranoid. Throughout the seventies and into the eighties, Williams continued writing, publishing a persona damaging but highly successful *Memoirs* in which he spent a great deal of time detailing his sexual exploits and far less time discussing his writing. By the eighties, he was largely thought to be a has-been. In 1981, his last play produced in New York City was panned by critics and Williams stopped writing plays altogether. In 1983, he died in the middle of the night, having scooped up two seconals with a bottle cap; he choked on the cap and died with his companion in the next room.

Though identified largely by his earlier, Pulitzer Prize winning work, critics are redirecting their attention to the newer plays, suggesting that those works may have been misjudged initially. Whatever the movement within scholarship, Williams has a permanent home as one of the finest American playwrights of the twentieth century and perhaps the best recognized for the wailing, hyper-masculine ("Stella!) Stanley Kowlaski and the coquettish and insane Blanche DuBois ("I have always relied on the kindness of strangers.").

The Story Behind the Story

Williams came into the theater scene at a time when much of Broadway played musical comedies or revivals of Greek plays. Because of the war-torn age, anxiety was high and the output of original playwriting generally low except for the efforts of Eugene O'Neill and a somewhat later, Arthur Miller. Williams enjoyed early success with his first play and it was during rehearsal of *The Glass Menagerie* that Williams began writing the first scene of *A Streetcar Named Desire*. He then called it "Blanche's Chair in the Moon" as he wrote over the winter of 1944–1945. He kept toying with the manuscript even after he submitted the 'finished' manuscript to his agent Audrey Wood in 1947.

After the runaway success of his first play, *The Glass Menagerie*, Williams found himself a much feted and confused young playwright. With the advent of his success, Williams moved from a hand to mouth existence to a champagne and caviar lifestyle. He found the success overwhelming and stultifying. He left New York City, heading first for St. Louis for an eye operation, where he claimed in "A Streetcar Named Success" that he was finally able to hear sincerity in people's voices again. He then left for Mexico where, in Chapala, he whiled away his time working on "Blanche's Chair in the Moon" which became "The Poker Game," which then became *A Streetcar Named Desire*. From the titles alone, Williams's ambivalence as to the main character is clear.

In February of 1947, Williams submitted the manuscript for *A Streetcar Named Desire* to Wood who worked with the recently divorced Irene M. Selznick, the producer, to get a director and actors for the play. Williams was particularly concerned with the choice of director. Based on Elia Kazan's work on *All My Sons*, Williams wanted Kazan who was not initially interested. His wife coaxed him into taking the project. Once Kazan came on board as director, Williams headed to Provincetown, Massachusetts to work on revisions of the play, leaving much of the casting to Kazan.

In the course of negotiations, Kazan demanded a great deal of control, leaving the artistic decisions almost exclusively to himself and Williams. Williams approved of the deal. Jo Mielziner was hired as scene designer based on his work on *The Glass Menagerie*. Casting was somewhat more difficult. Williams and Selznick met Kazan in Los Angeles to see Jessica Tandy star in another Williams play, *Portrait of a Madonna*; Williams was smitten and Tandy signed on as Blanche, leaving the all important role of Stanley still in the air.

Marlon Brando's "audition" is a thing of legend. Williams had left for the Cape and was happily ensconced when he received a young actor from Kazan's famous Actor's Studio. Kazan gave Brando twenty dollars for bus fare to Provincetown and sent him to read. Brando kept the money for food and thumbed his way up to the Cape. When he arrived, he fixed the plumbing and the electricity and then astonished Williams, who thought Brando gave the best reading he had ever heard. Williams immediately called to confirm Kazan's choice. Karl Malden (Mitch) came from the Actor's Studio and Kim Hunter (Stella) was suggested by Selznick.

Response to *A Streetcar Named Desire* was somewhat divided. In a vitriolic review, theater critic George Jean Nathan wrote, "His play ... remains largely a theatrical shocker which, while it may shock the emotions of its audience does not in the slightest shock them into any spiritual education ... His writing ... sounds almost altogether too much like a little boy proudly making a muscle" (Hurrell 90). Other critics raised similar issues, calling Blanche a common prostitute, arguing that the sexuality was coarse and inappropriate. Critic Harold Clurman felt altogether different and his views represent a much broader number of critics both past and present. He wrote of *A Streetcar Named Desire*: "Its impact at this moment is especially strong, because it is virtually unique as a stage piece that is both personal and social and wholly a product of our life today. It is a beautiful play" (Hurrell 92). He continues in his review to laud the play as "great theater" and "an original play on Broadway." The play won the New York Drama Critics Circle award, the

Donaldson Award and the Pulitzer Prize for Drama, the first play ever to win all three.

In 1951, the film version was released, retaining almost the entire original cast, with the exception of Jessica Tandy. Instead, an aging Scarlett O'Hara, actress Vivien Leigh became the Blanche of popular culture. Her fame as Scarlett certainly added authenticity to the role of Blanche, the aging Southern belle, and Leigh, Malden, and Hunter all won Oscars for their performances; the play won The New York Film Critics' Circle Award and Marlon Brando's method acting revolutionized the craft.

As the decades pass, the shock value of the play has dissipated but the obsession with its characters has not. At the Tennessee Williams Festival, men still gather annually in New Orleans to cry out for their Stellas and Blanche DuBois's famous line has found its way into popular culture, from community theaters to *The Simpsons*.

List of Characters

The **Negro Woman** is a friend of both Eunice and Stella, showing, in theory, that the races intermingled in the quarter. She also represents "reality" in opposition to Blanche's fantasy world. Her actions are generally avaricious and self-serving.

Eunice Hubbell is the upstairs neighbor and landlady of the Kowalski's. Her marriage is also troubled by violence which, like Stella, she accepts as part of life. She represents the character of the Quarter and the kind of life that Stella has chosen.

Stanley Kowalski is a blue collar worker of Polish descent, a former World War II soldier, and a man's man. He is a sexual predator and a happy patriarch of his own small kingdom. He is married to Stella, who he holds in a kind of sexual thraldom. He is also Blanche's primary antagonist, believing her to be a liar and a threat to the life that he has made with Stella.

Stella Kowalski is sister to Blanche and wife to Stanley. A former Southern belle, she fell in love with Stanley while he was in uniform, and left behind her upper-class roots to follow Stanley. His animal magnetism attracts her inexorably and she is carrying his baby. Throughout the play, she is torn between a desire to be loyal to her sister or loyal to her husband.

Steve Hubbell is the upstairs neighbor and landlord of the Kowalski's. He is also a close friend of Stanley's and a World War II veteran. He too shows the violent domestic space the Kowalski's inhabit.

Harold Mitchell (Mitch) is Stanley's best friend and Blanche's gentleman caller, her best chance for an escape from the life that she has made for herself. Mitch is the most sensitive of the men in the play. He lives with and cares for his ailing mother and harbours a deep attraction for Blanche and her wiles.

21

Ultimately, though he turns against Blanche, he feels in some way responsible for her madness.

The **Mexican Woman** is a blind old woman selling flowers for the dead. She appears as Mitch and Blanche engage in their fight. She represents a kind of blind prophet, foretelling Blanche's "death" as a descent into madness. She also represents the dead boy who was Blanche's husband.

Blanche DuBois is Stella's older sister, Stanley's antagonist and victim, Mitch's girlfriend, a former English teacher, a widow of a homosexual husband, and a seducer of young men. She is from an upper-class background and feels horrified by her sister's descent in class as well as her brother-in-law's animalistic and sexual ways. She possesses a delicate beauty that age is slowly stealing and she is desperate to snag Mitch to prevent herself from being alone.

Pablo Gonzales is a member of the poker players, another working class friend of Stanley's. He is also the person to whom Stanley most condescends, thereby mirroring Blanche's behaviour towards him.

The **Young Collector** is a young man whom Blanche tries to seduce and then thinks better of it. He represents the young men and the desire that has destroyed Blanche in the past.

The **Nurse** works largely in opposition to Blanche. She is a sturdy and stern character unlike the mentally and physically fragile Blanche. She manhandles Blanche, trying to get her to leave with the doctor.

The **Doctor** comes to represent the strangers from whom Blanche has received some small kindness in the past. He is her last hope for some sort of salvation, and she turns from the cruel nurse to the doctor, who as a man, might respond better to her wiles and thereby fulfil her need for safety and care.

Summary and Analysis

Critic Felicia Hardison Londre locates "the first indication of the play's brilliance in its title ... which signals the importance of theatrical metaphor in the work (Roudane 48). She notes that it links both the concrete with the abstract, the streetcar and desire and that it suggests the theme of a journey, both physical and emotional, and of transience as well as establishing a very specific locale (Roudane 48–49). The next thing a reader encounters is the epigraph from American poet, Hart Crane's "The Broken Tower" which immediately suggests a certain anxiety of influence. The desperate quest for love, and its fleeting nature, immediately sets the emotional stage of the play. That quest, whether for physical or metaphysical love, drives the characters of the play, particularly the DuBois sisters. But, the quote reflects most intimately Blanche, the character who entered the "the broken world/ To trace the visionary company of love, its voice/ An instant in the wind (I know not whither hurled)/ But not for long to hold each desperate choice." Love, for Blanche, is momentary, a choice most often born of desperation. Most of Crane's word choices suggest violence, posing love as a destructive force, but he still refers to love's company as visionary, making it simultaneously enlightening and devastating. According to critic Gilbert Debusscher, Williams always had the epigraphs to the play reprinted in the playbills for the audience. In this case, Debusscher asserts that the quote shows the past-present juxtaposition of Belle Reve as a lost false dream and Vieux Carre, Stella and Stanley's small apartment, as the threatening future. This dichotomy suggests that neither Stanley nor Blanche will have love for long (Roudane, ed. Debusscher 173). Thus begins one of the most influential plays of modern theater.

The overall structure is deceptively simple. Actress Roxana Stuart, who played Blanche, said, "the first four scenes are comedy; then come two scenes of elegy, mood, romance; then five scenes of tragedy" (Roudane 49). For director Elia Kazan, each scene of the play might be organized by "what Blanches wants, makes happen, or has happen to her" (Roudane 50). Others suggest that the play is split by sympathies—the first half for Stanley, the second for Blanche.

To begin the play, Williams first carefully sets the scene in one of the poor sections of New Orleans. As the set notes describe, the place has a sort of "raffish charm." In keeping with the dualities that began in the epigraph, here desire and death are side by side. The river moves silently along as the train rumbles down the other side of the area. Poverty pervades the area, as does the music of the bars. Underneath much of the play, a tinny piano plinks out the emotions of the scene; Williams refers to it as "Blue Piano" and it comes to reflect most strongly the emotional life of Blanche.

As **scene one** opens, people are gathered outside talking, enjoying the breeze, the races supposedly intermingling with ease. It is in this easy atmosphere that Stanley Kowalski and Mitch make their first entrance. Stanley carries with him a package of meat, its packing paper stained with blood. Both men wear work clothes, Stanley a bowling jacket. From the setting and their appearance, readers know that these two men belong to the blue collar working class. They are healthy, strong men, Stanley in particular. He yells for his wife, Stella, to come out on the stairs and he throws the meat up to her. Critics immediately make sense of this as Stanley enacting some sort of primitive rite of bringing meat home to the family as well as indicating Stella's titillation at her husband's virility. As critic Ruby Cohn writes, "Stanley has trained his wife to catch his meat, in every sense" (Stanton 49).

When Stella makes her entrance, Williams notes that she is "a gentle woman, about twenty-five, and of a background obviously quite different from her husband's." Stella's upper-class background has no currency here and she does not try to emphasize it. Instead, she embraces what she views as part of Stanley's masculine charm. When he throws the meat to her, she catches it and laughs. She is in his sexual thrall and willing to do much to keep him. She clearly enjoys his rough ways. In her mind, they are linked to his virility which attracts her deeply. Stella exits the scene, heading to the bowling alley to watch Stanley play. She leaves behind her upstairs neighbour and landlady, Eunice, who is speaking with an African-American woman. The two are the first to meet a bewildered Blanche DuBois, Stella's older sister.

Blanche's name has been the cause of much conjecture among critics. Some see it as a projection of purity, others see it as part of a game that Williams was playing with the censors. Critic Nicholas Pagan suggests that Blanche might reference the verb form of the word "blanche" reading it as per the Webster's dictionary definition, "to bleach by excluding light" (Pagan 66). Certainly, Blanche is a creature of the night, more prone to show herself in the gentle light of the evening rather than the full sun of the morning. He also suggests that it might refer to the unconsummated marriage between her and Allan Grey, a sort of pure marriage, bereft of sexual contact. Pagan also links this to the name "Blanche" colloquially used to express the idea of "white-washing, glossing, or more bluntly, lying"(Pagan 64). Critic Ruby Cohn suggests that it might refer to her obsession with men if the last name were anglicised. With each interpretation of the name, the theme of illusion recreates itself. Blanche's world is dying. It is the world of the Old South, dotted with decrepit plantations and ancestral homes, like the lost Belle Reve (Belle Reve is also problematic in that it does not agree in gender. It needs either to be Belle Rive—beautiful river—or Beau Reve, beautiful dream. Like its heroine, its name suggests ambiguity and subterfuge), and populated by romantic boys who were too weak to survive in the industrial world of capitalism and reality, like Allan Grey. Blanche DuBois is another fatality in the changing, post-war United States.

Her former profession as a schoolteacher also helps to reinforce some of the major contrasts between her and her antagonist, Stanley. As critic Alice Griffin writes, "Making Blanche an English teacher allows Williams full play for lyricism and literary allusions, which are quite in character ... Her long speeches, verbal arias, develop metaphors while building rhythmically to a climactic sentence." Stanley's speech is generally clipped and specific, reinforcing his interest in reality versus Blanche's obsession with illusion and allusion. It also sets up the game being played between Stanley and Blanche. Critic Leonard Quirino links Blanche's airs to the bluff of a card game. Blanche controls the game until Stanley catches on to her bluff, then, once he has the identity of her cards, he makes the move to destroy her (Tharpe 79).

Blanche enters uncertainly, dressed entirely in white. She is an aging beauty who should, as Williams says, "avoid a strong light." He also likens her to a moth, in her uncertainty and her seemingly pristine, delicate beauty. Quirino notes that the moth has often been the symbol for the soul, making Blanche's journey even more metaphorical (Tharpe 79). The moth analogy also suggests Blanche's compulsion. She moves inextricably towards that which will destroy her as the light will destroy the moth. For Blanche, the light takes the form of drink and men, especially young men as well as Stanley Kowalski. Characteristically, Williams also uses a series of symbols in describing the setting. Eunice first speaks to Blanche, asking if she's lost. Blanche, still bewildered by the squalor of what might be her sister's home answers with hysterical brightness, "They told me to take a street-car named Desire, and then transfer to one called Cemeteries and ride six blocks and get off at—Elysian Fields!" Appropriately, Blanche begins with desire, which foreshadows her devastation with her husband and then with the lovers that followed, leading to a kind of death (cemeteries) and finally to an afterlife (Elysian Fields). As the exchange progresses, Eunice assures Blanche that she is in the right place and the African-American woman heads off to the bowling alley to get Stella.

Critic Alice Griffin notes that this description of Blanche's trip also reveals the theme of a journey (Griffin 46). At this point, her journey has her between what critic Leonard Quirino sees as two equally uninhabitable worlds (Tharpe 80). Some critics claim that there is ambiguity as to which place is better, Belle Reve and its association with manners, debauchery and old southern traditions or Elysian Fields with its raffish charm, overt sexuality, and seething violence. Quirino claims, as Williams does, that neither approaches any sort of ideal. Rather, they are stops along a slow destructive trip for the fragile Blanche who was undone by the death and mannered immorality of the beautiful dream of Belle Reve, and is heading toward complete destruction in the Quarter.

Many critics link Blanche's journey to that of both Orestes and Orpheus. In the case of Orestes, she is travelling to escape the avenging deities who are horrified by the deed Orestes has committed, killing his mother to avenge his father. Blanche is haunted by the death of her young husband, Allan Gray, and finds herself chased by his memory. Orpheus famously made his way into the underworld and with the beautiful music of his lyre coaxed Hades to allow him to return to earth with his dead love, Eurydice. He was given only the condition that he must not look back at her before they reached the earth. He failed in this and lost his love a second time. Like him, Blanche has made her way into the underworld, a kind of dark night of the soul, and the music that swirls around her in memory, is as entrancing as that of Orpheus, and like him, she will fail her love.

Once in the apartment, Blanche effectively dismisses Eunice and sits in the kitchen trying to digest the reality of her sister's shabby two room apartment. Critic Frank Bradley writes that the apartment with its utter lack of private space, acts as an antagonist to Blanche. He asserts, "Nothing is safe from another person's scrutiny in such a space ... To lack privacy is to be exposed to multiple and often conflicting outside influences. To be public is to be impure" (Gross 55). The space also overlaps with that of the Hubbells, the upstairs neighbours who can be heard through the walls and the rest of the Quarter, which is emphasized by the scrim that separates the back wall of the apartment from the outside. A trick of light makes it utterly transparent. In such a space, Blanche is robbed of the familiar; instead, she is perpetually on enemy ground. Additionally, the use of the literary names that once grounded her have no currency here. Even they are unfamiliar and distant.

To prepare herself for meeting Stella and Stanley, Blanche

fortifies herself with the liquor that she sees in a closet, then carefully washes the tumbler to cover her tracks, suggesting a familiar abuse. She mumbles to herself, "I've got to try and keep it together," and the audience is once again reminded of her seemingly fragile state. Moments later, her sister comes around the corner, joyfully calling out to her. Blanche runs to meet her, repeating her name and calling her by her childhood nickname. Critic Nicholas Pagan sees the nickname as a part of Williams's complex symbology. "'Stella for Star' is the first of a number of astronomical/astrological references ... " (Pagan 64). Critic Normand Berlin claims that Stella for Star is another part of Blanche's fascination with light, only unlike Stanley, she cannot inhabit both the world of dark and the world of light (Tharpe 100). In other places, she references astrological signs, her own as the virgin, another part of her campaign to present herself as pure. As Blanche embraces Stella, she jabbers about the apartment, how Stella has fallen, insulting every part of her current living arrangement. Stung, Stella still offers Blanche a drink, thinking that her sister would be shocked to see how the working class live. Critic Bert Cardullo notes that this offering of a drink is a pattern of Stella's. Rather than communicate what she is feeling, Stella will offer a drink or make some other distancing gesture (Tharpe 141). She is either unwilling or unable to articulate her feelings.

The two circle each other in uneasy conversation as Blanche continues to denigrate Stella's life. Stella stays silent for most of the exchange, and Blanche comments on it. Stella claims that she has learned to be quiet around her, because she leaves no room for other voices. Stella, as she did in the past, turns into a kind of handmaid to Blanche, pampering and fetching for her.

Blanche invites Stella to question why she is there and then grows defensive. In an attempt to bolster her confidence, she comments on Stella's weight gain, and forces Stella to tell her how well she is looking. She tells Stella that she has brought nice clothes to meet Stella's friends and Stella struggles to explain that her friends are not what Blanche is expecting, that in this new life, new clothes are not necessary. Blanche continues blithely on, but her composure slips tellingly as she says, "I want to be *near* you, got to be *with* somebody, I *can't* be *alone*! Because—as you must have noticed—I'm—not very *well*." This is the first time Blanche slips in front of her sister, revealing how ill she is. Then, she is suddenly struck with fear at the notion that Stanley won't like her. Stella tries to calm her, but even she is dubious. She begins to say "You'll get along fine together, if you'll just try not to—well—compare him with the men that we went out with at home." Stella anticipates the collision of her aristocratic sister with her working class husband. Blanche continues chattering and the talk turns to Stanley, who Stella feels unable to describe, instead she shows Blanche a picture. This small act reinforces the fact that Stanley is an almost wholly physical presence, who must be seen and understood sensually. Stella points out that she met him in uniform, one of the great class levellers, which Blanche suggests is the only way that Stella could have fallen for him. Then Stella reveals that Stanley doesn't yet know that Blanche is coming and again Blanche begins to panic until Stella tells her that he is often away on business. Blanche assumes that this is good news until her sister rushes to dissuade her. Stella, enthralled by Stanley and his sexual nature, can't stand to be separated from him. Like her sister, Stella posseses a powerfully sensual nature that she has been able to direct towards Stanley. Blanche had no such mate.

Blanche finally gains the courage and tells Stella that Belle Reve is gone. Desperate to defend herself, Blanche launches an attack blaming Stella for leaving. Stella defends herself, saying that she needed to make her own life. Blanche details the deaths, the horror that she felt as they died, the relief of the funerals. Cardullo posits that it may well have been the "absence of truth and intimacy from life at Belle Reve is what drove Blanche into an early marriage and on the road to calamity, as is the stagnancy, the decadence, of postbellum plantation life what prompted her sister to opt for the vitality of New Orleans and marriage to a man whose virility could never be questioned (Tharpe 143). Critic Britton J. Harwood sees Blanche's steadfastness at Belle Reve as reflecting part of her ethics. He writes, "Loyalty—standing by someone who needs help—is Blanche's ethic" (Tharpe 112). Still, as she makes speeches about her loyalty to Belle Reve and its inhabitants, she also judges herself guilty in not coming to the aid of her dead husband. In many ways, Blanche does not know when to leave even as she sees situations disintegrating in front her as with Belle Reve. Wrapped in her own grief, guilt and fear, she fails to notice that Stella has begun crying until Stella excuses herself to wash her face. At this point, Stanley comes on the scene, bringing with him the racket of his constant talk, his noisy friends, and the bright color of his bowling shirt.

Blanche hears him initially speaking with his friends on the stairs. Williams made sure to give some foreshadowing within this portion of the scene. Steve, husband to Eunice and landlord, tells Stanley a get rich quick story, and Mitch quickly tells Steve to stop, that Stanley will believe it. The men know that Stanley is a big believer in things that he has heard, that he believes in the authority of the expert. To add humour to the scene, Steve and Eunice have a little tiff. They are a shadow of Stella and Stanley, their bicker about being home on time represents the everyday squabbles of couples up and down the block, and serves to relieve some of the tension that the sisters have built up in the scene. Stanley heads to his own apartment.

Unlike Blanche, Stanley stands on no ceremony. He is a sort of hard working everyman with whom the audience initially sides. He is the cliché male, working hard, playing hard, etc. When he enters the room, he speaks loudly, sure of his authority, particularly in his own home. He ascribes to the notion that a man's home is his castle and he rules accordingly. He also differs from Blanche particularly in speech and action. Critic Ruby Cohn writes, "The hard consonants of Stanley Kowalski contrast with the open vowels of Blanche DuBois. As opposed to her mothlike whiteness, Stanley moves in a world of vivid color; Williams compares him to *a richly feathered male bird*." ... On stage, Stanley's physicality contrasts with Blanche's ready verbalizations (Stanton 49–50)." Critic Alvin B. Kernan is quick to note that Stanley is a realist who trusts only his own senses (Bloom 11). For this reason, he is easily swayed by rhinestones, believing them to be diamonds, and easily enraged when he has been fooled by his own eyes. His is a hard world, a capitalistic race with which the idealistic Blanche is necessarily at odds.

He also has his own distinct mode of articulation according to Griffin: "Stanley's idiom is made up of army and conventional slang, trite expressions, street grammar, curses and grunts like "huh?" His sentences are short. But there is humor too, however crude, as well as an unquestioning trust in authority, such as the Napoleonic code. Using all of these marks of character, he goes one step beyond; Stanley has a poetry of his own that is particularly his; it is heightened, alliterative and rhythmic (Griffin 63)." In addition, Stanley is proud of his place in Elysian Fields, his place on the bowling team, among his friends. He does not begin the play as Blanche's enemy. As critic Britton J. Harwood points out "Blanche raises Stanley to consciousness and to vindictiveness, because she makes him ashamed" (Tharpe 109), thereby making an enemy of him.

When he enters the room, Blanche pre-empts him and introduces herself. Unfazed, Stanley, asks where Stella is, then continues making small talk, introducing little earthy jokes into the exchange, being convivial and welcoming. Unfortunately, the questions that he asks—about Blanche's home, her husband—upset her already delicate state and the music of the polka can be heard. Williams uses music to indicate the moments when Blanche begins to lose control and move into memory. The polka is music particular to the memory of her husband. When Stanley probes a little deeper, Blanche cuts him off entirely, collapsing, claiming that she will be sick.

The first scene firmly establishes the essential class differences between Stanley and Blanche, with Stella firmly set in the middle. In some ways, the two are fighting for control of Stella. Stanley wants his life to remain as it is, and Blanche wants someone to be with her and protect her, and the last person that she has is Stella. Stella herself is torn and her ambivalence affects the other two as they vie for her attention. Additionally, the two are used to represent a more thematic division. Critic Nancy Tisschler writes of the battle between

Blanche and Stanley as a battle between the Romantic Ideal and the real, respectively. "Stanley's view of Blanche parallels society's view of the artist. He resents the implicit judgement on his own habits of mind and life. He resents the intrusion into his world of this alien voice. And he feels threatened by the strength behind the veneer of weakness ... Williams allows the more complex antipathy between the lover of the ideal and the lover of the real to be his motive for destruction" (Stanton 168).

In **scene two**, it is early the next evening and the sisters are preparing to go out. Stella has arranged dinner at Galatoire's and a show. She is intent on keeping Blanche away from the poker game, believing, rightly, that Blanche will find it low class. Already, it is clear to Stanley that Blanche is unsettling his neat world. Rather than having a warm meal, Stella has assembled a cold plate for him and left it in the ice box. Stella urges Stanley to compliment Blanche when she gets out of the bath. Williams is careful here to show the intimacy between the couple. Stella has brought her concern about her sister to her husband, and he immediately thinks to protect her, although he does so at the price of Blanche. After he asks, she explains that Blanche has been through an ordeal and lost Belle Reve. Stanley is immediately suspicious and he enters the bedroom to ravage Blanche's trunk, pulling out faux furs and costume jewellery, convinced that Blanche has scammed them both. His anger reflects his inability to garner those things for his own wife, his obsession with the look of things rather than their reality, and his conviction that people are trying to put one over on him. Stanley spends a great deal of energy courting experts, always claiming that he has friends who can verify his claims that the jewellery is real. His fear of being swindled, and being thought less of a man as a result of it, colors his relationship with Blanche, making it still more tense. He claims the Napoleonic code, a further construct of authority, in defense of his behaviour, but Stella is uninterested.

In the midst of this domestic quarrel, Blanche can be heard singing in the background and splashing in the tub. She has retreated to her purification ritual of the bath. Williams uses the bath throughout the play as an escape for the overwrought Blanche. She disappears into the bathroom to be made pure again, to rinse away her sins, her guilt, and her sexual attractions. Here, Williams uses it as a powerful antithesis to the adult relationship and discussion of Stella and Stanley. Critic Alice Griffin suggests that the purification of water might also be a reference to Lethe, the River of Oblivion, from which the dead would drink to forget their lives on earth (Griffin 68). Quirino furthers this analysis by including Stella as "one of the happy dead" (Tharpe 81), drugged after sexual consummation with Stanley.

Disgusted by Stanley's distrust, Stella urges him to leave the room with her, but Stanley is determined to confront his sister-in-law. His tantrum has tipped the balance in favor of Blanche, and Stella is, for the moment, sympathetic with her sister rather than her husband. Blanche comes out of the bathroom in a red silk robe, a siren of sorts, and she begins flirting with the riled Stanley who believes this is another way of her patronizing him. She prattles on about his card party and asks him to button her dress then spritzes him with her atomizer. She asks about her trunk and pretends to be unconcerned when Stanley claims that he was helping to unpack. She plays for a compliment and Stanley grows increasingly annoyed but also sexually titillated. Critic Ruby Cohn sees her behaviour as part of her larger role as the Southern Belle, one to which she has became dedicated in the hopes of securing a man (Stanton 47). Nonetheless, it is artifice, one which will eventually envelop her completely. Blanche is playing with fire, believing that she can control her sexual brother-in-law through his own attraction. Critic Alice Griffin asserts that Blanche's flirtatiousness represents Blanche wielding one of her only weapons—her sexuality (Griffin 57). She is quickly proven wrong when Stanley, determined to discuss Belle Reve, tells Blanche that he likes a woman who lays her cards on the table, reinforcing the gaming metaphor.

Stella tries to call him to join her, then she calls Blanche who asks Stella to run to the pharmacy to get her a lemon coke. Stella reluctantly goes and Stanley begins his diatribe on the

Napoleonic Code. Blanche maintains her cool until in unearthing the paperwork, Stanley spies some letters and grabs them. The letters are from Blanche's dead husband, and as she snatches them back, they fall to the floor. She falls to her knees undone, and blurts out that she will have to burn them, now that he has touched them. Genuinely baffled, Stanley asks what they are, and Blanche responds, "Poems a dead boy wrote. I hurt him the way that you would like to hurt me, but you can't! I'm not young and vulnerable any more. But my young husband was and I—never mind about that! Just give them back to me!" Stanley returns them to her, beginning to realize that she has insulted him, but Blanche, exhausted now, continues talking, offering him the papers from the bankers and the lawyers.

Blanche launches into her famous speech about the loss of Belle Reve due to the "epic fornications" of generations of men who eventually bankrupt the family and lost the house. Blanche laughs bitterly and hands the papers to him, saying "I think it's wonderfully fitting that Belle Reve should finally be this bunch of old papers in your big capable hands! ... " Stanley bristles, claiming a lawyer friend who will verify their contents, then he lets it slip that Stella is pregnant. Immediately, the blue piano music grows louder as Blanche slips into a kind of reverie, dreaming about the baby that will come when Stella comes back to the house. Blanche exclaims over her, and for the first time, expresses some small happiness that Stanley is in the family, saying that his blood may be what they need after losing Belle Reve. As the two women exit, Blanche asks which way to go and then laughs, saying, "The blind are leading the blind." Neither sister can yet see the parallels between the epic fornications of the past and the inherited sexual nature that will destroy Stella's marriage and Blanche's sanity.

Scene three begins later that night, with the men assembled at Stanley's small apartment playing poker. Williams particularly sets the scene with "lurid" colors, highlighting the sensual nature of the group. Like Stanley, all of the men are highly physical, in the prime of their lives. Only Mitch is slightly more refined. When the scene starts, Stanley is already irritable, due to a turn of bad luck. Beside him, Mitch begins to make noise about leaving, worried about his bed-ridden mother at home. According to Williams scholar, Philip C. Kolin, Mitch is representative of a whole sub-set of Williams' suitors, all characterized by suffering from "interrupted/incomplete sexuality, branding them as representatives of a desire that is fathomable, disappointing (Voss 133). Unlike the other men, the only woman waiting for him is his mother. He bears the stamp of a mama's boy, though he longs for a female, he is still not man enough to have one. Kolin claims that even his work in the "spare parts department" emphasizes his incompleteness (Voss 136).

Around the corner, Blanche and Stella are arriving home; it is 2:30 in the morning and the poker game rages on. When they enter, Blanche asks the men not to stand, emphasizing immediately the class difference between her and her brother-in-law who tells her that no one is going to stand anyway. Stella formally introduces her husband's friends to her sister, showing that in this moment, she is siding with her sister, believing Stanley to be rude. He suggests that they go and stay with Eunice upstairs, but Stella refuses which Stanley answers by slapping her hard on the thigh, his violence foreshadowing what is to come. Furious, the two women exit into the bedroom and pull the curtain shut between the two rooms. Unnerved, Blanche says that she will bathe, another attempt to purify herself in light of what is happening around her. Just as she intends to go in, Mitch comes out of the restroom, wiping his hands on a towel. His gaze immediately goes to Blanche; he is clearly fascinated and attracted. He and Stella exchange small talk while Blanche observes Mitch. After he leaves to re-join the other men, she turns to her sister, stating that he seemed different. Stella responds positively, Mitch is a good man and he cares for his ailing mother. Blanche lightens the moment by asking if he is a wolf, and Stella laughs, settling into girlish gossip with her sister as they change out of their clothes.

While they are talking, Stella confides that Stanley is the only one of the men going somewhere, and like his attraction for Stella, it is based on his animal charisma and drive. As she speaks, Blanche steps into the light, wearing only a bra and slip, her silhouette distracting Mitch from the poker table. Stella warns her to step out of the light, and Blanche pretends not to have noticed, but as Stella steps into the bathroom, Blanche turns on the radio, then deliberately moves back into the light, stretching herself like a cat and dons her red silk wrapper.

Immediately, the already annoyed Stanley demands that Blanche turn the radio off, the men try to placate him, telling him to "let the girls have their music" but Stanley sees the radio as the women undermining his place of authority in the house. To prove who is master, he storms into the other room, turns off the radio and glares at Blanche. Undaunted, Blanche meets his gaze squarely, another instance of their sexual chemistry. He returns to the kitchen where the men are arguing over naming the game. They ask Mitch to verify what was said, but he has been too distracted, looking through the curtains. He decides to sit the game out, saying he has to use the bathroom. The other men make snide remarks about him leaving with his winnings, joking that he will put them in his piggy bank. Kolin interprets his desire to be dealt out of the masculine realm of the card game as another way in which Mitch's incomplete masculinity is characterized (Voss 136). His devotion to his mother causes the other men to infantilize him. He exits to the bedroom where he stops just inside the curtain, seeing Blanche who tells him that the bathroom is occupied.

Awkwardly, Mitch explains that they have been drinking beer, and Blanche, in a flirtatious confrontation, says she hates beer. In so doing, she immediately puts Mitch even more off-kilter, strengthening her command of the situation and of him. She asks him for a cigarette and Mitch immediately produces a silver cigarette case which Blanche admires. Eager to show that a woman has loved him in the past, and to garner her sympathy, he urges her to more closely examine the box's inscription, written by a dead girl. Even in Mitch's one epic romance, he was unable to complete the union as the girl died before he was able (Voss 136). It also highlights the sort of operatic romance that attracts Mitch to Blanche. He still admires the high drama of lost love and the damsel in distress, so when Blanche plays the part, he is an easy mark. As he tells of his dead love, Blanche feels connected to Mitch, and she begins to flirt more seriously, setting herself up as a paragon of virtue, explaining how little she generally drinks, and how tonight, due to circumstances, she was forced to drink a little more. The suggestion that her inhibitions might be a little lowered intrigues Mitch and he tells the men to deal him out of the game. She explains the origins of her name. Here, Williams again uses symbolism. Blanche DuBois, meaning white woods, suggests purity in this context as Blanche spins it. Critic Ruby Cohn, however, notes that "even her translation is a fantasy. Blanche is past her spring, and the purity of Blanche-white is undermined by the thicket of DuBois-woods. Anglicized, Blanche's name is DuBoys, and under her chaste surface, Blanche lusts for boys" (Stanton 46). Here, even the names foreshadow what is Blanche's fall.

Continuing her ruse, she claims also to be Stella's younger sister, another small duplicity by which she establishes herself as eligible rather than desperate. She then asks him to help her by putting the paper lantern over the light bulb. Eager to have something to do, he complies, and Blanche says, "I can't stand a naked light bulb, any more than I can a rude remark or vulgar action." According to critic Normand Berlin, "That she must cover the light and live in the shadow indicates her twilight condition and her attitude towards life: 'I don't want realism. I want magic!' Blanche lives between light and dark, avoiding the truthful glare of the former and unable to attain the latter" (Tharpe 100).

To mask her reasons for coming, Blanche claims that she has come to care for Stella who has not been well. The two continue flirting, both establishing their status as single by the time Stella exits the bathroom. When she sees her sister, Blanche turns on the radio and waltzes around the room. Entranced, Mitch sways to the music "in awkward imitation, like a dancing bear." Again, Mitch's shyness and awkwardness comes to the forefront and in the face of it, Blanche becomes even more animated, convinced that she can seduce Mitch, partially by overwhelming him.

When Stanley hears the radio again, he goes ballistic. Blanche has seduced his best friend from the poker table, helped to instigate an argument between him and his wife, and undermined his authority by turning the radio back on. He storms into the bedroom and throws the radio out the window. Critic Jacqueline O'Connor sees this as a precursor to Stanley's other reactions to the highly verbal Blanche. He does not care for extraneous noise, and when he hears it, "he disposes of it (O'Connor 62). Embarrassed and angry, Stella demands that the men leave, and before they can move, Stanley, convinced that Stella is emasculating him further, stalks into the kitchen, drags her out of sight and hits her. Stunned, Blanche exclaims that Stella is pregnant, doubling the horror and spurring the men to action. Seeing Blanche's upset, Mitch takes control and tells the men to bring Stanley into the bedroom. It takes two men to get him into the room, where suddenly he goes limp and the men "speak quietly and lovingly to him and he leans his face on one of their shoulders." Clearly, Stanley and his friends are close. This moment of the scene reinforces the bond between Stanley and Mitch, helping to explain the motivation for Stanley's protective instinct toward his best friend. Shaken, Stella exclaims that she wants to go away and Blanche goes to Mitch and demands her sister's clothes. Because of Stella's reliance on her in this moment, Blanche is strong, believing that now she will not be alone; Stella has been returned to her and she is ready to do all that she can to protect her sister. Mitch finds the clothes and hands them to Blanche, repeatedly saying that, "Poker should not be played in a house with women" thereby reinforcing his old-fashioned chivalrous attitude towards women.

Stanley asks what happened, as if coming out of a trance. The men quickly reassure him that he just lost his temper. Mitch still angry, tells them to put him in the shower, and they do, even though they have to force him under its spray. Once they have him in there, they scuttle out, wanting to avoid more conflict. Stanley wanders, forlorn, back into the bedroom and realizes that Stella has left him. Cacophonous music rises up and Stanley leaves the room, climbing down the back stairs to the street where he begins wailing for his wife. The fact that Stanley immediately knows where Stella has gone suggests that this has happened before, and in talking to Eunice, who tells him to go home, she reveals that it has happened before, the last time involving the police. Stanley ignores Eunice, calling insistently for Stella, who moved by the need in his voice, creeps down the backstairs to join him. When the two come together on the stairs, the full degree of Stella's enthrallment is evident. In the stage directions, Williams wrote, "they come together with low, animal moans. He falls to his knees on the steps and presses his face to her belly, curved with maternity. Her eyes go blind with tenderness as she catches his head and raises him level with her." Almost mesmerized by his magnetism, she lets him bear her into the apartment.

A few moments later, baffled and confused by the commotion, the violence and her missing sister, Blanche steps out onto the landing, then down the steps where she stares at her sister's apartment. She gasps when she realizes that Stella has gone back. In this moment, Blanche realizes that she has lost Stella to Stanley; she realizes how powerful his pull is, and she begins to look around for some other sanctuary. As she does, Mitch comes around the corner. He asks if all has calmed, and Blanche, unable to contain her shock, tells him that Stella has gone back to Stanley. Mitch is unfazed. For him, as for the majority of the street, this is fairly commonplace. All of the actions of the friends and the neighbors indicate that they have dealt with this before. He tries to minimize the event, saying that Stanley and Stella are crazy about each other, but Blanche is unconvinced. He offers her a cigarette and she makes noise about being improperly dressed. Mitch hushes her protests, saying, "That don't make no difference in the Quarter," and Blanche becomes finally fully aware of what makes no difference in the Quarter: violence, sexuality, propriety. She becomes aware too, that Mitch might be her best chance of protection from the life that she has come to know with her sister and brother-in-law. Portentously, she leans close to Mitch and says, "Thank you for being so kind! I need kindness now."

Scenes three and four help to set up a pattern for Stanley

according to critic Bert Cardullo. With Stanley's drunken temper firmly established, the eventual rape of Blanche will seem not so much destined as part of Stanley's behaviour when drunk, thereby making it slightly less horrific because it seems unpremeditated (Tharpe 138). **Scene four** begins early the next morning with an indolent Stella, sexually satisfied and smug, lolling in bed. In stark contrast, Blanche, unnerved and sleepless, hesitates before entering her sister's room, unsure of what she will find. The aftermath of the night before litters the apartment, spilled cards, Stanley's pyjamas. When Blanche sees Stella in the bed, she rushes in to greet her, both relieved and resentful. As Blanche fawns over her, demanding to know what she was thinking returning to Stanley, Stella draws away from her, unaccustomed to someone commenting on the night before. In the past, life has simply gone on, settled by sex. Critic Leonard Quirino notes that Stella, unlike the displaced Blanche, seems to have no problem moving between the person she was at Belle Reve and the person that she is in the Quarter (Tharpe 81). Unlike her sister, Stella adapts to the environment as needed. She has little investment in the idea of herself as a Southern Belle. Stella gets out of bed and reassures Blanche that Stanley was sorry and that he had made it up to here. Appalled, Blanche keeps pushing, but Stella puts the whole thing down to Stanley's passionate nature and reveals how much that thrills her. Quirino references earlier moments to heighten the sisters' sexuality. He claims that Blanche sees it like the rattle-trap streetcar, decayed, unsettling, unsteady, unreliable. Stella, on the other hand, responds to Stanley's thrown meat of the first scene with a gasp and a giggle. She is held in thrall by sex. As Quirino notes, neither is particularly healthy (Tharpe 84).

At her sister's insistent worry, Stella becomes slightly irritable, claiming that she has forgotten how dramatic Blanche can be, but Blanche presses on, urging Stella to leave her current life, claiming that Stella is still young and can make a life for herself. Clearly, Blanche still believes that a new life will have to come from a man, as her comments about youth and attractiveness attest. Stella emphatically states that she does not want to get out of her marriage, and she turns to cleaning up from the night before, which enrages Blanche. She can't stand to watch Stella clean up after Stanley's tantrum. This famous speech posits brutality versus culture, a battle which Quirino sees as really being a part of the battle between body and soul. Blanche is the "soulful" one while Stanley and Stella are lulled into sleepwalking through their lives by drink, gaming, and sex (Tharpe 86). Importantly, Blanche too is intrigued and burned by the same fires that singe her sister and brother-in-law; however, she is ill-equipped to handle them due to the Belle Reve legacy of death and loneliness.

Scene four also introduces the depth of Blanche's mental condition when she declares that she will write to Shep Huntleigh, an old beau with whom she no longer has contact, and have him save them by setting them up in business. Stella scoffs, but Blanche becomes increasingly convinced of her plan and attempts to send a wire in which she states that she and her sister are in desperate circumstances. Stella laughs in her face, and Blanche continues to scratch out a plan, scouring her purse for money to find that she only has sixty-five cents to her name. Stella tries to share some of the apology ten dollars that Stanley has given her but Blanche refuses it and Stella becomes curious about her sister's lack of money. Blanche's lack of funds, and therefore lack of autonomy, are part of Williams' larger commentary on the fate of women without means. As critic Jacqueline O'Connor writes, "As we saw in both *Streetcar* and *Portrait of a Madonna*, Williams believes that a woman without economic means may end up at the state asylum (O'Connor 83).

The two continue dancing around the problem of Stanley which Stella tries to excuse as Stanley at his worse, but Blanche counters claiming, "I saw him at his best! What such a man has to offer is animal force and he gave a wonderful exhibition of that! But the only way to live with such a man is to—go to bed with him! And that's your job—not mine!" Blanche reveals that she too feels attraction for Stanley, although she recognizes that she cannot act on it and without acting on that attraction, she has no way to control him. Stella, when urged to leave by

Blanche, claims that "there are things that happen between a man and a woman in the dark—that sort of make everything else seem—unimportant." For Stella, the physical passion trumps the more daily concerns of domestic abuse; for Blanche, desire is something far less attractive. "What you are talking about is brutal desire—just—Desire!—the name of that rattle-trap street-car that bangs through the Quarter, up one old narrow street and down another ..." says Blanche. When Stella asks her if she has "ever ridden on that street-car?" Williams is pushing the metaphor, forcing audiences to remember the play's beginning and where it ended, in death. Blanche responds truthfully that it "brought [her] here."

Stella finally submits to Blanche's pleas to speak plainly, and just as Blanche launches into a vicious account of Stanley, he appears in the kitchen, unnoticed. He remains to hear the entirety of Blanche's outburst. She claims he is a beast; he is common; he is an ape, the missing link. His poker game is a group of apes coming together. She urges her sister, "Maybe we are a long way from being made in God's image, but Stella—my sister—there has been *some* progress since then! Such things as art—as poetry and music—such kinds of new light have come into the world since then! In some kinds of people some tenderer feelings have had some little beginning! That we have got to make *grow*! And *cling* to, and hold as our flag! In this dark march toward whatever it is we're approaching ... *Don't—don't hang back with the brutes!*" Critic John M. Roderick believes that this speech "underscores the class struggle and the social tensions which lie behind much of the conflict in the play" (Tharpe 116). Cardullo reads the exchange as Blanche's attempt to bond with Stella against Stanley; Blanche needs and wants a helpmate (Tharpe 143). When Blanche finishes, Stanley heads quietly back out under the cover of a passing train. He yells from outside alerting the women to his presence. Stella, overwhelmed by affection and loyalty for him after her sister's speech, runs to him and embraces him "fiercely." He smiles over Stella's shoulder at Blanche. Some critics claim that it is a smile of triumph. He knows that Stella has chosen him in spite of Blanche's commentary. Cardullo suggest that it is merely relief; his wife still loves him and was not swayed by her sister's commentary (Tharpe 144). As the scene ends, the blue piano plays again, giving the last comment to the inhabitants of the Quarter. Blanche has lost another round.

The time is a few days or weeks later, Blanche has been on a number of dates with Mitch and things seem to be progressing nicely. Blanche is seen fanning herself in the bedroom, waiting for Mitch, as she listens to a fight between Steve and Eunice. While vaguely comic, the fight over fidelity and Steve's hitting Eunice, closely mirrors the marital relations of Stanley and Stella. When Stella asks if Eunice has called the police, Stanley answers that she's gone for a drink, Stella responds that her action seems more practical than alerting the authorities. The audience understands again that this is typical of life in the Quarter.

When Steve comes down from the upstairs apartment to ask where Eunice has gone, Stanley directs him to the bar. They come back a few moments later, holding tightly to each other, clearly over their earlier squabble, again shadowing the Kowalski's tumultuous relationship. In the interim, in the midst of a tense exchange, Stanley casually drops a bomb on Blanche, asking if she knows a Shaw. Immediately, Blanche tenses and tries to talk her way out of the corner that Stanley is determined to put her in.

While she dances around his questions, Stanley tells her that he has a friend who goes in and out of Laurel who will verify the rumors. He leaves a stricken Blanche in the bedroom and tells Stella that he will meet her at the bar. Blanche pounces, panicked, upon Stella, demanding to know what she has heard about her sister. Stella tries to reassure her and Blanche tries to explain herself without revealing any factual information. She says merely that she "wasn't so good the last two years or so, after Belle Reve had started to slip through my fingers." Stella offers a general rationalization but Blanche stops her. The audience begins to see how truly desperate she is and gains a sense of what she has planned. Blanche says, "I never was hard or self-sufficient enough. When people are soft—soft people have to got to shimmer and glow—they've got to put on soft colors, the colors of butterfly wings, and put a—paper lantern over the light ... It isn't enough to be soft. You've got to be soft and attractive. And I—I'm fading now! I don't know how much longer I can turn the trick." Her terror of aging and what she perceives as its subsequent nature, that of being alone, appears quite clearly. The edges of her mental state are beginning to fray. Stella chooses to ignore it and brings her sister a soda to calm her. Again, Stella provides a beverage rather than emotional support. Blanche is still so unnerved that she asks for a shot in the coke, which Stella provides, claiming she loves to wait on her sister because it feels just like home that way, offering another insight into what life at Belle Reve must have been like.

Stella's care for her overwhelms Blanche and she presses her mouth to her sister's palm in a gesture of desperate affection. She then promises that she will leave, that she knows she is ruining the relationship between Stanley and Stella, but at the same time, she can't keep herself from blaming Stanley for her feeling of unwanted. While she is talking, Williams adds telling gesture to the scene. Blanche's hands are too shaky to hold the coke without spilling it; Stella adds the shot to the soda and it fizzles over. Blanche gives a hysterical little scream, shocking Stella. She tries to cover her mounting hysteria by claiming it stained her skirt. Then she claims that it is all worry over Mitch. While Blanche is setting the pace for the relationship and refusing physical affection from him, she also shows that she desperately fears losing him and the kind of life that he might offer her. She says to her sister, "What I mean is—he thinks I'm sort of—prim and proper, you know! [She laughs out sharply] I want to *deceive* him enough to make him—want me ..." When Stella asks if she wants Mitch, Blanche bursts out, "I want to *rest!* I want to breathe quietly again! Yes—I *want* Mitch ... *Very badly!* Just think! If it happens! I can leave here and not be anyone's problem ..." Blanche sees herself almost as the last dying person from Belle Reve, but unlike the others, she is unwilling to let her life be a burden on Stella. She wants a way out from that existence. Moved, Stella kisses her sister and reassures her that Mitch will marry her even as Stanley bellows from the street for his wife and friends. But, the exchange isn't all positive, before she leaves, Stella warns her sister not to take another drink. Clearly Stella is now aware of her sister's drinking problem.

After the Kowalskis and the Hubbells have left for the evening, Blanche sits back in the chair to recover herself and as she does, a young man comes to the door, collecting money for the newspaper. Blanche, attracted, invites the young man in for a drink as she explains that she is not the lady of the house. The boy then moves to leave, but Blanche stops him, asks for a light and begins to flirt with him, asking where he went in the rain. He tells her that he stopped in the drugstore for a cherry soda. Charged with sexual tension, Blanche tells him, "You make my mouth water." The young man is clearly discomfitted, but Blanche presses on as the sound of the blue piano rises into the scene. She compliments him, then crosses the room and kisses him before sending him on his way, murmuring to herself that she has to let him go, has to be good and "keep [her] hands off children." Williams uses the dialogue here to explain Blanche's dismissal from the school. While she is still in a daze over the boy, Mitch rounds the corner, and Blanche goes back into character, pretending to be a French coquette as she tells Mitch how to court her. Critic Kolin sees this as another part of Mitch's ineptitude. As the desired party, the newsboy, leaves, Mitch bumbles in with his tired romantic gesture of roses, a few minutes after Blanche has already been aroused. As per usual, he is a sloppy second arriving a little too late (Voss 136).

Scene six begins later that same evening, around two in the morning, outside of the apartment building. Mitch carries with him an upside down statuette of Mae West, suggesting that they spent the evening at an amusement park, as per the stage directions. Kolin views this as further evidence of Williams's efficient use of symbols. Importantly, the doll is upside down rather than right side up, suggesting that he has not been acknowledged as a winner in the shooting gallery, another reference to phallic inability. Rather, West is representative of the sort of female he could never win, one infinitely more skilled in the ways of the world than he, much like the woman that he is with now (Voss 137). Unfortunately, Mitch is unable to distinguish that. When they enter, the scene, Blanche looks exhausted and Mitch depressed. The two stop outside the apartment building and awkwardly wait for the other to indicate what will happen next. Mitch apologizes for the evening's lack of fun, and Blanche apologizes for her inability to rally. She hands Mitch her purse in a gesture of trust. Kolin links the purse to Chaucer's allusion—the purse is representative of the vagina, and the key of the phallus. Prophetically, Mitch has difficulty, picking through the purse until he finally finds the key to her trunk, thinking it the key to the door. Blanche corrects him, and identifies the key herself. Her intervention highlights his sexual ineptitude (Voss 137). Ultimately, he knows neither how to hold a woman (Mae West) nor how to consummate a relationship (key/door). She then mentions that she shall soon need it as she will be packing to leave. Mitch asks why, and Blanche just says she has overstayed her welcome. Her response urges him to ask her for her hand, but Mitch is oblivious. He finally opens the door, then shyly asks if he might kiss her. Blanche, tired of his ineptitude, asks why he has to ask. Mitch answers honestly, in stark contrast to Blanche, that he doesn't know whether she wants him to or not because of a night at the lake where she slapped his hands away. Intent on continuing her facade as a lady of high virtue, she says that she might get lost were she to give in to his overtures. Her response both makes her sound sexually charged and demure. When Mitch offers another earnest response, she bursts out laughing, hurting his feelings, then looking for liquor in the dark, while suggesting that Mitch go into the vacant bedroom.

Mitch moves to turn on a light and Blanche insists instead that they set the place like a stage, pretending that it is a little French cafe. She flirts in French and when Mitch admits that he can't speak it, she asks, in French, if he would like to sleep with her, then exclaims, again in French, that it is a shame that he can't understand her. Cohn notes that her "question has wider cultural currency than that French language, and

Blanche takes a risk for her poor little joke—the risk of destroying her pure Southern Belle image in Mitch's eyes" (Stanton 47). This is one of the few scenes where Blanche seems aware that she is playing the role of the Southern Belle rather than actually being one. Cohn links her obsession with her role with her descent into madness. They move into the bedroom where Blanche tries to get Mitch to remove his jacket, but Mitch confesses that he is embarrassed of the way he sweats. Blanche tries to reassure him, then comments on the material of his jacket, which Mitch insists is good for his build. He then talks about his workout routine, settling finally on the topic of his weight, which he realizes is boring Blanche. In an attempt to enliven the conversation, he then asks what she weighs. She tells him to guess, and he asks if he can lift her. She agrees to it, and Mitch lifts her, then keeps his hands on her waist, ready to kiss her. She calls him Samson, another allusion to a man sapped of his strength by a woman, then she teasingly demands her release, still playing the coquette, and tells him to be a gentleman. But, Blanche's heart is not in the teasing, she wants Mitch to make a more decisive move, and even as she explains her old-fashioned ideals again, she can't help but roll her eyes at Mitch's obtuseness. To cover his own awkwardness, he coughs, which Kolin reads as "male capitulation and isolation after a failed attempt (Voss 138).

After the awkward silence following her dismissal of his advances, Mitch fumbles for conversation, asking finally where Stella and Stanley are, and then suggesting that they should all go out. Blanche sees a chance to discover more about Mitch's loyalties to Stanley and more about what Stanley might have told Mitch about her. Mitch tries to avoid the questions, shrugging her off by saying that Stanley has mentioned little, although his tone suggests that is patently untrue. Blanche keeps pressing the matter, insisting that Stanley is insufferable, that he hates her and acts rudely just to bother her. Mitch tries to remain neutral, and finally offers the weakest of assurances, "I don't think he hates you." Blanche rushes to convince him, "He hates me. Or why would he insult me? The first time I laid eyes on him I thought to myself, that man is my executioner!

That man will destroy me, unless—." Blanche's pronouncement is a powerful foreshadowing of events. In her hysteria, she recognizes still that Stanley poses the greatest threat to her, because of his violence, his unpredictability and his desire to be rid of her. Before she can go on, Mitch interrupts her, to ask her age. Again, Mitch shows that he is completely out of sync with Blanche. He ignores her impassioned commentary with a non-sequitor, asking her age. Blanche hedges, not wanting to reveal her age and hurt the facade that she has created for Mitch. He insists that his mother wants to know. Blanche takes that as a good sign and asks why his mother wants to know. Mitch tells her that his mother wants to see him settled, suggesting implicitly that Blanche might be the person with whom he settles.

Blanche confides that she too is lonely, that she has loved someone who died, the same person that she alluded to when Mitch told her of the dead girl who gave him the cigarette case. She pours herself another drink and begins to tell the story of her late husband, Allan Gray. In this monologue, Williams reveals the root of Blanche's neurosis, a confrontation between Blanche and the homosexual Gray, who killed himself immediately thereafter. The exchange referenced a chance meeting that led to Blanche seeing Gray and an older man in flagranté. Though the three pretended it had never happened, the knowledge proved too much for the young and desperately in love Blanche. She told Gray that he disgusted her, and he left the dance floor, ran to the pond outside the club, and shot himself through the head. The melody of the Varsouviana haunts the memory, and Williams used the device of this music to cue the intensity of Blanche's memory and her rising hysteria. She is unable to forgive herself for Gray's death and unable to recover from it on her own. As she tells the story, her body sways and shakes giving away her anguish. Moved, thinking of his own lost love and longing for Blanche, Mitch offers, "You need somebody. And I need somebody, too. Could it be—you and me, Blanche?" Startled and saved, Blanche exclaims, "Sometimes—there's God—so quickly!" She believes that Mitch will marry and protect her; indeed, as critic

Jacqueline O'Connor notes the melody of the Varsouviana dies away when Mitch embraces Blanche, suggesting that he can be the one to save her from the memory of her dead husband (O'Connor 48).

Scene seven begins later, in mid-September. The scene is set with decorations for a birthday party, Blanche's, a Virgo birthday, the sign of the virgin, an irony not lost on Blanche herself. Stanley walks into the apartment where Stella puts the finishing touches on the decorations. After Stella reveals who the decorations are for, he asks where Blanche is, mocking her frequent escapes to the hot tub and scolding Stella for catering to her whims. He then begins updating her on his investigation of Blanche, telling Stella that Blanche did, in fact, stay at the Flamingo Hotel, that she had relations with a number of men, that she was listed as "out-of-bounds" for the local military unit, that she was fired as a teacher for pursuing a seventeen-year-old boy. Throughout, Stella voices her disbelief and her fury with Stanley, but he remains adamant, telling her that he checked and checked again, that it is all true. During his speech, he makes side remarks mocking Blanche's facade of gentility.

In counterpoint, Blanche's singing reinforces her worldview as she croons, "It's only a paper moon. Just as phoney as it can be—But it would be make believe If you believed in me!" Berlin links this paper moon to the paper lantern and the paper boy, all of which reflect "Blanche's gossamer grip on reality" (Tharpe 100). Critic Jacqueline O'Connor writes of the scene as further evidence of Stanley and Stella's collusion against Blanche. According to O'Connor, "The final exchange between the two, before Blanche emerges from the bathroom, indicates that Stanley and Stella both realize that if Blanche cannot stay with them, and cannot return to her life in Laurel, something unmentionable awaits her in her future:

Stella [slowly]: What'll-she-do? What on earth will she-do!
Stanley: Her future is mapped out for her.
Stella: What do you mean? (I, 367)

... Although he is not specific, this exchange signals what is to come, for it is the Kowalskis who decide Blanche's fate, not Blanche herself (O'Connor 44). She interrupts their conversation to ask Stella for another towel. Dazed, Stella complies, but Blanche sees her face and knows that something is wrong. She retreats back to the bathroom, her only refuge for the moment.

As Stanley reveals all, Stella latches on to one of his offhand comments about Mitch, demanding to know if he has told his friend about Blanche. Stanley looks slightly shamefaced in the glow of Stella's anger, but he recoups. Stanley believes it an act of loyalty to tell his friend, bowling team partner, war buddy and co-worker about the women that he is considering. Stella defends her sister, explaining about Allan Grey, but Stanley remains unmoved, even when Stella demands to know if Mitch is "through with her." He finishes his revelations by announcing to Stella that Blanche will be leaving on Tuesday. He has bought a bus ticket which he knows in light of her past, is essentially a death sentence. After dropping that news, he yells at Blanche, again, to get out of the bathroom. When she comes into the room and sees Stella's face, her own turns into a mask of terror and Williams's disjointed piano begins a breakdown, signifying the beginning of Blanche's utter unravelling as well as Stella's sorrow over losing the sister she once knew (Pagan 59). It should be duly noted that the breakdown begins before the rape. It is not only Stanley's sexual violence that pushes Blanche over the edge.

Scene eight begins forty-five minutes later as the three sit around the table in a grisly facsimile of a family. A fourth seat, meant for Mitch, is empty. To break the discomfort, Blanche urges Stanley to tell a joke, but it is clear from her overly bright demeanour that she is wound tightly. Stanley goes on the offensive reminding Blanche that she doesn't like his stories. Determined to fake a pleasant atmosphere, she tells her own story, laughing too loudly at its end as Stella tries to look amused and Stanley, ignoring her, begins to gnaw on the leftover pork chop. Blanche makes a comment and Stella, furious and hurt over what she feels is Stanley's betrayal, yells at him for eating like a pig, then orders him to clean his greasy face and hands and help her wash the dishes. For Stanley, this is the final straw and he hurls his plate to the floor, scaring both Blanche and Stella. He begins to rant against them and the ways they have put him down, calling him, "Pig—Polack—disgusting—vulgar—greasy." He asserts that every man is a king in his own home and that Blanche and Stella better remember it. Clearly, Stanley's diatribe smacks of the patriarchal control that was the province of both the upper and lower classes. In either case, in such a system, the man is in charge, even if that means the destruction of everyone around him as with the "epic fornications" of the DuBois family. Stella cries as he leaves the kitchen.

The display further convinces Blanche that something is terribly wrong and she questions her weeping sister, sure that Stella knows why Mitch has not made it to the party. Blanche decides to call Mitch since Stella won't tell her. Stella tells her not to, but Blanche needs to know how much damage has been done. She heads for the phone in the bedroom and Stella heads out the porch to berate her husband for hurting Blanche so badly. Stanley tries to soothe her with the promise of sexual satisfaction when Blanche leaves, emphasizing again the strong sexual pull in their marriage. Above them, Steve and Eunice can be heard laughing together, as if to emphasize the marriage the Kowalskis once had, and Stanley believes, will have again, once Blanche is gone. Slightly calmed but still saddened, Stella tells Stanley to come back inside and they join Blanche, who tries to put on a brave front, saying that she will not be taken for granted. She is trying to break up with the absent Mitch before he can break with her. Stanley complains about the steam from the bathroom and the phone rings. Blanche starts to rise, still half-believing that Mitch will call and explain himself. Instead, it is one of Stanley's friends from the bowling team. When he hangs up the phone, he turns to Blanche again, and offers her a small envelope for her birthday. Blanche takes it uncertain as to whether it is a peace offering or a trick. When she opens it, she blanches and Stanley tells her that it is a bus ticket to Laurel and the Varsouviana begins to play, signifying her mental fragility. Stricken, now that her only remaining safe place has been taken from her, Blanche runs into the bedroom, looking like a pursued animal. She runs into the bathroom and begins retching. Immediately, Stella begins reproaching Stanley on her sister's behalf. Stanley moves into the bedroom to put on his bowling shirt. Stella is stunned at his insensitivity, but he begins to tell her how he did it for them, how Blanche has ruined their marriage, making Stella think of him as an ape.

As he continues, the similarities between Stella's sexual drive and that of Blanche are apparent. Stanley says, "When we first met, me and you, you thought I was common. How right you was, baby. I was common as dirt. You showed me the snapshot of the place with the columns. I pulled you down off them columns and how you loved it, having the colored lights going! And wasn't we happy together, wasn't it all okay till she showed here?" Again, Stanley, like his wife in an earlier scene, emphasizes their sexual connection. Like Blanche, Stella is led powerfully by her libido, although for different reasons. The union with Stanley made it possible for her to be a sexual woman without societal disapproval. As Stanley talks, entreating her, Stella goes into labor. Stanley turns to her and sees her expression, and immediately asks what's wrong. Stanley returns to being her loving husband and supports her arm, whispering reassurances in her ear. They leave behind an ill and mentally fragile Blanche who doesn't even know they've gone.

Scene nine starts later in the evening. When the scene opens, it is clear from both the music and the clothes that something is seriously wrong. Blanche sits huddled on a chair that she has covered in a delicate green and white striped fabric. She has been drinking in her scarlet dressing robe and the "Varsouviana" is at a fever pitch in her mind. Outside the apartment, Mitch approaches, unkempt, still in his work clothes. His ringing the bell startles a clearly distraught Blanche out of her own thoughts. When Mitch calls out his name through the door, Blanche immediately hides the liquor bottle and splashes her face with powder and cologne, to wipe out the results of drinking. When she opens the door, Mitch pushes past her, ignoring her mouth raised for a kiss. In desperation, Blanche buzzes with mania around Mitch, scolding him for the way that he has treated a lady with his absence and his dishevelled appearance. Mitch stares at her in drunken amazement, then asks her to turn off the fan. Eager to return to his good graces, she complies, then offers him a drink. The state of her deteriorating mind is evident as she stills hears the sound of the waltz which she actually mentions aloud, saying that she is waiting for the gun shot, that it always stops after the gunshot. Notably, Mitch's presence no longer has the power to stop the sound of the waltz for her. Allan's haunting death has become a part of her present as her mind unravels.

When she offers him a drink, Mitch is reminded of the reason that he came in the first place, and he declines the drink, saying he doesn't want any of "Stan's liquor." Blanche tries to tell him that it is hers, but defeats herself moments later, when she pretends that she doesn't know what Southern Comfort is. Fully cognizant now of the number of lies that she tells, Mitch just watches her "contemptuously." She continues to flitter, talking about the wonders that she has worked with the apartment and Mitch tells her that Stan has accused her of drinking all his liquor over the summer. While she works on her denial, Mitch begins to prowl the room, reminiscent of Stanley. He comments on the darkness of the apartment, which Blanche claims she likes. Convinced suddenly that even the lighting of the apartment is a ruse used to make a fool of him, he demands to see Blanche's face in the light, claiming that she never lets him see her during the day. Enraged, he tears the paper lantern from the light bulb. Blanche gasps, feeling herself inextricably exposed. Blanche asks why he has done that and he responds that he wants a plain look at her, something real. Blanche bursts out in what many believe to be a credo taken straight from Williams himself: "I don't want realism. I want magic! [Mitch laughs] Yes, yes, magic! I try to give that to people. I misrepresent things to them. I don't tell the truth, I tell what *ought* to be truth. And if that is sinful, then let me damned for it! *Don't turn the light on!*" Mitch turns the light on and stares at her; she covers her face. Her speech reveals many truths, the reasoning, however convoluted behind Blanche's whimsical talk, the connection of light to tragedy, the full brightness of love and the dousing of the light with Allan's death. Anything too bright can only bring the memory back, and with it the guilt that has flayed Blanche.

Mitch turns the light off. Unlike Stanley, he has a hard time maintaining the torture of a woman he loved. He tells her that he wouldn't have minded her age. It is the sort of vanity lie that he can understand based on the way that he sees women, but the hypocrisy regarding her sexual history, he cannot forgive, telling her "I was fool enough to believe you was straight." For critics interested in queer theory, many believe that this is the unveiling of Blanche as Williams, a kind of transgendered character and the question of straightness refers not so much to telling the truth as to sexual orientation. It represents the coming out of the transgendered homosexual within the text (Pagan 66). Coupled with the reading of her name as the anglicised DuBoys, the character of Blanche might easily be read as representing that of the gay male.

Blanche bitterly asks if it was Stanley who suggested that she wasn't "straight." Mitch tells her yes, but then explains that he checked, that he had faith in her until he spoke with all of Stanley's sources, one of whom Blanche claims was a jilted lover, and therefore bitterly spreading tales about her. Thoroughly disillusioned, Mitch gives more names and the name of a hotel, the Flamingo. Realizing that she has lost him, she begins to correct his story. The hotel was the Tarantula Arms, where Blanche claims to have "brought my victims." She tells her story finally, that after Allan's death she sought protection, safe haven in the arms of strangers, even a seventeen-year-old boy. Like a thwarted criminal she tells all, that she believed that Mitch might have been exactly the protector that she needed now that her youthful appeal was gone. She calls him, "a cleft in the rock of the world that I could hide in!" Mitch, unable to take it all in, repeats like a simpleton, "You lied to me, Blanche." She counters with "Never inside, I didn't lie in my heart."

Just as Blanche is fighting for the life that she might have had, her past comes around the corner, this time as an old blind Mexican woman selling flowers and crowns of flowers for the dead. Hearing her vaguely, Blanche opens the door, and immediately feels frightened, calling out, "No, no! Not now! Not now!" She sounds as if the ghost of Allan Grey has come back to exact his payment of her and the Mexican woman comes to represent death, of the soul, the mind, the body. As this mysterious figure of death wanders away, the polka music begins and Blanche turns back into the apartment, talking to herself, about the legacy of her family, death and bills and silence, being unable to mention the death that was in the room for most of her life. She begins to explain that after all of the work and the suffering that broke her, she turned from death to desire, to the soldiers who would call up to her from the lawn. She would sometimes meet them, to feel the opposite of the rest of her life. Outside, the Mexican woman can still be heard calling softly, reminding Blanche of the death at Belle Reve, a parody of a beautiful dream. The music of the polka suddenly dies away as Mitch's hands on her waist returns her to reality. He claims that he wants, "What I been missing all summer." Seeing his desire, Blanche tries one last time to deal her sexuality for marriage, demanding that he marry her.

In a crushing putdown, Mitch removes his hands and says, "You're not clean enough to bring in the house with my mother." For Kolin, this is another way that Mitch expresses his incomplete manhood. Still unable to stand up for his own feelings, he uses his mother to rid himself of Blanche (Voss 139). Crushed and furious, Blanche demands that he leave. When he doesn't move, she begins to threaten, hysterically, that she will yell fire, which she does, sending a terrified Mitch scuttling out the apartment and into the night. Once he is gone, Blanche sinks to her knees and a slow, blue piano begins.

In the hours that follow Mitch's hasty departure, Blanche has drunk steadily and pulled her trunk out to the center of the bedroom where she has begun packing. Williams writes that "a mood of hysterical exhilaration came into her and she has decked herself out in a somewhat soiled and crumpled white satin evening gown and a pair of scuffed silver slippers with brilliants set in the heels" (122). To finish the ensemble, she tops her head with a tiara and begins speaking "as if to a group of spectral admirers." Even without Stanley present, Blanche has already begun to unravel. As she talks to her admirers, she happens to glance into the hand mirror and sees herself, prompting her to smash the mirror facedown onto the vanity. Shaken, she tries to rouse herself and as she does so the audience sees Stanley at the corner, dressed in the vivid colors of his bowling shirt. The emphasis on color directly connects to Stanley's sexual confidence, reminding readers of the colored lights that he smashed during the honeymoon. Even the music of the scene is Stanley's—a honky tonk that continues throughout, a little raunchy, a little unschooled. When he enters, Blanche immediately asks about Stella. Stanley, pleased and expansive, tells her that the baby won't come until morning; he has been sent home to sleep. Immediately, Blanche pinpoints the danger of the situation; the two are to be alone together.

Stanley teases her a little, confirming that it is just the two of them, unless she is hiding someone under the bed. Blanche, so accustomed to lying her way out of trouble, immediately goes into her dance, claiming a wire from Shep Huntleigh, that she claims includes an invitation for her to join him on a cruise. Stanley is immediately suspicious and tries to get her to give him all the details, so that he can investigate them later. He asks if Shep is the one who gave her the fur pieces and the diamond tiara. Blanche corrects him, explaining that the furs are fake and the tiara made of rhinestones; Stanley no longer cares, although his obsession with these goods and their relative worth emphasize again that Stanley only cares to see what that which is sensually understandable. For him, the jewel that shines is a diamond. He is also largely unconcerned about her lies at this moment. If she claims the millionaire, then Stanley is going to hold her to it, and send her to Dallas. Whatever the case, she will be gone and he will have a new baby.

Stanley begins to take his shirt off and Blanche demands that he shut the curtain if he is to undress. She is desperately trying to keep some propriety between them. He laughs her off, saying that he will undress no further then begins rooting around for the bottle opener for the beer that he has brought home. Desperate to distract them both, Blanche begins to rattle on about a cousin who could open beer bottles with his teeth. Ignoring her, Stanley uncaps the bottle, which overflows, and he lets it pour over his head, then offers Blanche a truce, saying "Shall we bury the hatchet and make it a loving-cup? Huh?" Blanche declines, which Stanley shrugs off, saying that it is a night to celebrate for both of them with their mutual good luck, then he steps into the bedroom to get his pajamas. His entrance into the room with its clear connotations of sex disturb Blanche and she demands to know what he is doing. He withdraws his silk pajamas; he tells her that the brightly colored garments are good luck, worn on his wedding night. Blanche sees them, quite rightly, as a symbol of his libido.

He moves out of the bedroom and continues talking about how he will celebrate when he hears it's a boy, another subtle reference to the patriarchal positioning of the male over the female. Unnerved by his good humor, Blanche starts to try to one up him with her own, talking about how overjoyed she will be to have privacy again. Stanley pricks her asking if she really thinks that the oil man "is not going to interfere with [her] privacy any?" Blanche takes offence and begins to launch into one of her favorite speeches, about how much of a gentleman Huntleigh as a representative of the mannered boys of the Old South versus the unmannered, animalistic men of New Orleans. She exclaims, "A cultivated woman, a woman of intelligence and breeding, can enrich a man's life— immeasurably! I have those things to offer, and this doesn't take them away. Physical beauty is passing. A transitory possession. But beauty of the mind and richness of the spirit and tenderness of the heart—and I have all those things—aren't taken away but grow! Increase with the years! How strange that I should be called a destitute woman! When I have all of these treasures locked in my heart. [A choked sob comes from her] I think of myself as a very, very rich woman! But I have been foolish—casting my pearls before swine!" This outburst shows some of the greatest fears held equally by Williams and his character. Both fear growing old and becoming unattractive to men. Blanche fears poverty, knowing that without the ability to catch a man, with her career in ruin, that she is destined to struggle in poverty unless she can figure something out quickly. She also exclaims what she wishes were true, that wealth of the spirit were enough to save her. Unfortunately, in the dichotomy between the reality of the Quarter and that of Blanche's romantic illusions, neither is a viable space for her with her casual references to Shakespeare.

What Stanley hears in the speech is not her desperation, but another aspersion cast against his character. She has made him an animal again, a pig. Then she goes on to confirm that not only is Stanley a swine, but his best friend is as well. Caught up in her own passion and self-righteous indignation, she lies about Mitch, claiming that she broke it off with him, that he was heart-broken, so much so that he came back to repent the stories of Stanley's that he had repeated about her. She claims to be unable to forgive him because "Deliberate cruelty is not forgivable. It is the one unforgivable thing in my opinion and the one thing of which I have never, never been guilty." Her comments are revealing because Blanche does blame herself for being cruel, albeit not deliberately, nevertheless, it is her cruelty to her late husband for which she cannot forgive herself.

She then claims that their backgrounds are too different to be compatible, again playing the aristocracy card. Her comments about class and manners enrage Stanley and he begins to mount his offensive, interrogating her about the wire. Confused, Blanche begins to trip over the lie and Stanley moves in to make his point, accusing her of more "lies and conceit and tricks!" After making her look at her deception, he forces her to look at her appearance, from her mangled gown to her cheap tiara. He asks her, "What kind of queen do you think you are?" reinforcing Pagan's assertion that Blanche be read as a disguised homosexual character, this time in drag. Stanley continues his assault, congratulating himself on his ability to see through her and her various Southern Belle affectations, he finishes his speech by laughing at her pretension and coming into the bedroom.

Blanche immediately senses the threat of physical violence and orders him not to enter the bedroom. As her fear heightens, all around her "lurid reflections appear on the wall ... The shadows are of a grotesque and menacing form." As she tries to regain her composure, Stanley moves into the bathroom and Blanche tries to call Shep Huntleigh. In her panic, she begins to believe her own story. Without an address, the operator can't help her and hangs up, leaving Blanche to scramble for another plan of escape. Behind her, the wall that blocks the apartment from the street has dissolved and the reality of the inequity around her is everywhere. A prostitute is being chased by a drunk; they struggle before a policeman's whistle breaks it up. The prostitute leaves her purse behind and the Negro Woman of the first scene returns to root through the bag. Blanche tries to combat this reality with her fiction. She tries to dictate a wire to the imaginary Huntleigh, never considering that she might have to come up with a way to escape that does not involve a man rescuing her. As she makes her frantic attempts, Stanley comes out of the bathroom, vivid in his bright pajamas, a sexual predator. He knots the tie at the waist of his pajamas, reinforcing the theme of imprisonment and stares at Blanche. Helpless, she stares back until the phone begins to beep from being off the hook. Stanley crosses over to her and puts the phone back on the hook and stares at her, grinning, waiting for her to make the next move. As he waits, the sound of a train overwhelms the apartment and Blanche crouches with her fists over her ears to try to drown out the noise. Once it's gone, she rises again and tells Stanley to let her get by him. He invites her to do just that, stepping back one pace from the doorway. Blanche knows that he is still within striking distance and she tries to get him to stand further away. He refuses, telling her she can get by. At this point, Blanche can no longer see any alternatives. She knows that she has to escape and that getting by him is the only way to do that.

Stanley goads her, "You think I'll interfere with you? Ha-

ha!" Beneath the scene, the blue piano has begun, and Blanche turns back towards the bedroom, but lurid shadows rise up around her and she can hear "inhuman jungle voices". Stanley moves towards her, his tongue between his teeth, a visual omen of what sexual violence and imprisonment is about to take place. Stanley has begun to actively consider a specific plan of violence, muttering, "Come to think of it—maybe you wouldn't be bad to—interfere with ..." His approach forces Blanche to retreat back into the bedroom. Trying to hold her ground, she warns him not to come closer, then tries to threaten him with "something awful," but Stanley laughs at her, suspecting it to be another game. Cardullo claims that Stanley is acting not so much out of malice as out of attraction and sexual frustration. Since Blanche's arrival, his sexual life has been squelched and with the news of Blanche's indiscretions, she becomes fair game for his advances (Tharpe 138–139). In this game however, Stanley with his bulk and lucidity clearly has the upper hand. Feeling herself cornered, Blanche says "I warn you, don't, I'm in danger." She can articulate her experience but there is no one there to hear it. She breaks a bottle on the table and brandishes at him. Stanley asks why she did it and she says to twist the ends in his face. He looks at her wonderingly and states that he thinks she'd do it. Stanley begins to see this as part of a violent game that has been brewing between them. When Blanche moves to defend herself, he says, "Oh! So you want some rough-house! All right, let's have some rough-house!" implying that Blanche, through her behavior leading up to the night has asked for this kind of treatment. According to Cardullo, "he is reacting playfully to what he considers her momentary and obligatory, extravagantly affected resistance to his advances" (Tharpe 139).

He bolts at her, turning over the table and she tries to hit him with the bottle, but he grabs her wrist, forcing her to drop the bottle, saying, "Tiger—tiger! Drop the bottle top! Drop it! We've had this date with each other from the beginning!" For Stanley, her desperation only heats his desire to overpower her. Pushed into a corner, Blanche lashes out like an animal, finally behaving in a manner conversant with this reality, but her efforts fail. She drops the bottle top and falls to her knees, beaten. Stanley plucks her from the ground and carries her to the bed. Around them, the music of the Quarter rises, reinforcing the sense of Blanche being utterly overwhelmed not only by Stanley but the world that contains him. Critic Arthur Ganz writes that Stanley's persecution of Blanche puts him in the strange position of also being the avenger of Blanche's homosexual husband. He writes, "Although he [Stanley] is Williams's exaggeration of the Lawrencian lover, it is appropriate from Williams's point of view that Kowalski should to some degree be identified with the lonely homosexual who had been driven to suicide ... But however gratifying it may be to identify the embodiment of admired male sexuality with the exiled artist and thus by implication with the exiled homosexual, the identification must remain tenuous. Kowalski, though an avenger, is as guilty of destroying Blanche as she is of destroying her husband (Stanton 128)." Blanche, in this instance, here at the Vieux Carre, is the exiled, the lonely party. She has almost become Allan Gray.

Leonard Quirino likens the plot to another famous story outside of the play, that of "Tereus, Philomela and Procne—the rape of the visiting sister-in-law by her brother-in-law in the absence of his wife" (Tharpe 87). As Quirino clarifies, though no dead child is served to Stanley, Blanche loses her ability to speak of the event because Stella chooses to believe that her sister is lying in order to continue living with Stanley. Though Blanche's tongue is not cut out, it might as well be.

Scene eleven begins as a day time mirror of the evening poker game of scene three. The men and their game dominate the kitchen; the women are sequestered in the bedroom, Blanche readying and calming herself in the bathroom, Eunice and Stella packing the last of Blanche's garments. A few weeks have passed since the rape, and in that time, Stella has chosen to believe Stanley rather than the admittedly unbalanced Blanche, though Stella is still deeply torn. The survivor in her chooses Stanley. The scene is book-ended by the talk of the men and the game.

Stanley boasts making his hand and Pablo curses his luck in Spanish. Stanley tells him, "Put it in English, greaseball" mirroring in his condescension, exactly those traits that he most hated in Blanche (Tharpe 91), then begins his speech on luck, believing in one's own luck, how it is the only thing that will get one through. He takes for his example a maneuver in the war, out of five men he was the sole man to make it out, just as he is the sole survivor in the battle between him and Blanche. Still, his battle here was not without repercussion. As he blathers on celebrating his prowess, Mitch can barely tolerate the machismo, bleeting out, "You ... you ... you ... Brag ... brag ... bull ... bull." Again, Mitch fails to articulate himself in moments of emotional stress, furthering Kolin's belief that he cannot complete himself, even in language (Voss 136). He knows only that a woman he once loved is broken and that he and particularly Stanley are to blame. Stanley ignores Mitch's anger, pretending not to know what is wrong with his friend.

While the men play cards, Eunice comes from upstairs, where she has put the baby to sleep. She brings Stella some grapes, an excuse to check on Blanche, and particularly Stella. As she passes through the kitchen, she calls the men brutes for playing when Blanche is about to be committed. Again, Stanley pretends ignorance, determined not to lose the status quo within his apartment and his life. Eunice crosses into the bedroom where Stella asks after the only uncomplicated person in her life—the baby, the only third person who can live companionably with Stella and her husband. Eunice assures Stella that the baby is fine and then asks after her charge. Stella says Blanche is bathing, again using the bath as a purifying rite to keep her calm and good in the face of the debauched poker players. Stella tells Eunice that she has lied to Blanche to get her packed. She has told her that Shep Huntleigh is coming, effectively using Blanche's own insanity to trap her in the apartment a little longer.

While the women talk, Blanche opens the bathroom door and tells Stella what to lay out for her, the yellow silk with a sea horse pin and a bunch of artificial violets. Blanche has not wholly given up on the idea that she might woo a suitor into marrying her, but typically, her flowers are fake, lacking in scent and the sea horse is a creature under the water, an idealized place for Blanche where everything is clean and nothing cruel. She shuts the door after issuing her request and Eunice and Stella once again can speak openly, a direct contrast to the way in which Stanley and Stella can speak to each other. Stella worries that she has not done the right thing; Eunice reassures her, asking, "What else could you do?" Here again, the patriarchal nature of the South at this time in history plays a major role. Blanche has no one to go to. She has no other family. She can no longer work in teaching and no man wants to marry her. Stella can only send her to an institution or into the street. Despite its brutality, the institution can help Stella to believe that what Blanche has told her about Stanley's assault is a lie, and it will put her somewhere relatively safe where Stanley and Stella are no longer responsible for her. Stella even articulates her central dilemma: "I couldn't believe her story and go on living with Stanley." Additionally, as O'Connor points out, Blanche has set the precedent for Stella's disbelief. In her efforts to maintain her façade as a southern belle, she has told any number of small lies (O'Connor 63). Still, Stella's response completes the battle between reality and illusion. In order to continue living in reality, she, like her sister, must chose illusion in order to function.

Stella too is caught in the broader web of social necessity. Were she too leave Stanley, she too would have no place to go, no income, no security, no one to care for the baby. Brutal though he is, Stanley is a good provider for her and the baby. With him, they will eat, have health insurance, live in relative comfort and hopefully prosper. Without him, the prospects are bleak. Eunice, another woman intimately familiar with the bounds of being female in a patriarchy, speaks as a survivor, saying, "Don't ever believe it. Life has got to go on. No matter what happens, you've got to keep on going." Stella remains with Stanley, not so much because she loves him, but because she can see no other choice. He is a matter of survival for her and the baby, though Stella's affections have shifted. She can safely be enthralled with the baby, and suffer no societal misfortune for it. Her passionate nature, unlike her sister's, can be redirected without fault.

After the brief exchange, Blanche pokes her head out of the bathroom and asks if the coast is clear. Stella assures her, and tells Eunice to compliment her. Stella's comment to Eunice illustrates the fact that Stella knows that her sister has not completely disappeared and become a nameless straitjacket. Though the curtains are shut, Blanche asks about them as the noise from the poker game filters into the room, heightening her anxiety. When she comes fully into the room, the Varsouvania begins to rise and Blanche is frenetically bright as she talks with the other two women who buzz around her, trying to keep her calm. She asks if Shep Huntleigh has called and in the kitchen, upon hearing her voice, Mitch's arm slumps down. Stanley smacks him and says, "Hey, Mitch, come to!" to bring his attention back to the game. His voice breaks through Blanche's careful vivacity. Shocked, she mouths his name and Stella nods. All of her artifice is gone and she looks suddenly confused when she asks, "What's going on here?" Her voice alerts Stanley in the other room and he rises to go into the bedroom. Steve stops him with a cautionary hand on his arm and Mitch slumps lower, terrified and complicit. As Blanche demands an explanation, Eunice and Stella try to shush her, a routine they have perfected in trying to dodge Stanley's ire. They finally calm her slightly, by telling her how wonderful she looks, that she will be going on a trip. Galvanized, Blanche urges them to help her so that she can escape the apartment which she keeps referring to as a trap. The women comment on her jacket, hoping to keep her distracted, and she tells them that the jacket is "Della Robia blue. The blue of the robe in the old Madonna pictures." With the reference to the Virgin Mother, Williams seems to indicate that Blanche too is her own kind of purity, not of the flesh, but of the spirit. She is, as she claims, never deliberately cruel. She plucks a grape from the bundle that Eunice brought down earlier, and asks if it has been washed, then makes a comment that the cathedral bells are the only clean thing in the Quarter. Even now, she too has been jaundiced. Though she arrived in white, she is leaving in color, a pale yellow, a figurative statement about the affect of her time there. She tries to leave but the women tell her to wait until the poker game has broken up. Then, like Tennessee Williams before her, she indulges in a reverie around her own death, how she will die at sea, holding the hand of an attractive young ship's doctor, all because of an unwashed grape. Williams claimed that he wanted to be buried at sea at the place closest to where Hart Crane, the poet whose epigraph began the play, was buried. Blanche too wants that, to be delivered into the cleansing waters of the ocean via a pristine white bag. The color of the ocean will remind her of her first lover's eyes.

As she rhapsodizes, the Doctor and the Nurse arrive. Their bearing speaks of official and officious business. They are plain and severe, clearly not from the Quarter or the old South of Belle Reve. They are something harder, more matter of fact, nearly mechanical. When they hear the doorbell, Stella presses her fist to her mouth which Blanche notices and asks, "What is it?" Eunice saves the moment, saying that she will see who it is. Blanche convinced by the charade wonders if it is someone for her, and Eunice confirms that it is for her. She wavers between excitement and terror, which the faint sound of the Varsouviana reinforces, she asks if it is the gentleman from Dallas. Eunice claims that it is. Postponing the moment, Blanche says she is not quite ready, and Stella tells Eunice to make them wait. Drums sound softly as the tension begins to mount. Blanche claims she is not fully packed and Stella tells her that they are waiting. Blanche immediately picks up on the plural, then tries to figure out who the woman with him might be. She tries to guess her position by the clothes that she wears but can come up with no reason why he might be accompanying Shep. She is beginning to see the cracks in the story and cannot contain her fear. As she steps into the kitchen, by rote, she tells the men not to get up, all of them stand, save Mitch who stares at the table, unwilling to see what has happened to Blanche. She steps out onto the porch, sees the doctor and gasps. Terrified by his presence and the lies that she has been told, she tries, ironically, to seek Stella's help, telling her that the man is not Shep then dart back into the apartment for safety as the sound of the Varsouviana begins to pick up. Stanley is the sole person seemingly unaffected by what is going on. He continues to shuffle the cards. In the kitchen, Mitch won't look at her still, though the other men stare. She tries to make it to the bedroom, but Stanley stands as if to block her way in a replay of what had happened the night of the rape. He again uses his body to intimidate her.

Behind Blanche, the matron has followed her. Unexpectedly, it is Stanley who gives Blanche a temporary out, asking her if she has forgotten something. Wild, she takes the excuse that he has offered and runs into the bedroom, wild disjointed voices seeming to follow her. The voices replay the night of the rape, intensifying the audience awareness of Blanche's tangible terror. Stanley tells the doctor that he better follow Blanche. The Doctor tells the nurse to get her, and the Nurse begins to advance on Blanche. The Nurse says that they will pick whatever it is up later, Stanley asks what it is, then tells her, "You left nothing here but spilt talcum and old empty perfume bottles—unless it's the paper lantern you want to take with you. You want the lantern?" He rips the lantern off the bulb and waves it at her. She gasps, terrified again of the light and all of its terrors—the memory of Allan, of Mitch's near assault, Stanley's assault, her own aging and helplessness. The Nurse then steps towards her purposefully and Blanche tries to run by, aware that she is in a trap. All the men jump up, ready to corral her, and Stella, undone, runs to the porch, unable to watch her sister being wrangled like an animal.

Eunice embraces Stella on the porch as she weeps for her sister, begging Eunice to help her, to stop what is about to happen. She tries to break from Eunice, but Eunice is a part of the plan too. She holds Stella and tells her to ignore what is happening to Blanche, just as she is to ignore what Stanley has done to Blanche in the past. Mitch too tries to do something to save Blanche. He makes for the bedroom but is blocked by Stanley. Enraged by his friend's callousness, Mitch takes a swing at Stanley who pushes him down to the table. Mitch, ever the ineffectual one, collapses, sobbing, at the table. Inside the bedroom, the Nurse holds Blanche as she tries to claw her way out of the Nurse's confining embrace. Unaffected, the Nurse tells the doctor that Blanche's nails will need to be trimmed, reducing the terrified woman to a wayward child or spitting animal. She then asks if she should use the strait jacket. The Doctor says no, and instead, he takes off his hat and becomes human, speaking softly, "Miss DuBois." In the midst of the violent chaos, Blanche immediately responds to the manners reminiscent of the life she once knew. "She turns her face to him and stares at him with desperate pleading." With this stage direction, the Doctor sees that Blanche will come easily if she is treated with some degree of kindness. Blanche asks him to make the Nurse let go, then he pulls her up from the ground, and escorts her, like a suitor, from the bedroom. She turns to him and says, most famously, "I have always relied on the kindness of strangers." The irony is two-fold. First, one might expect to rely upon one's family for support; however, in this family of death and epic fornication, little kindness is possible. In some ways, Stanley has certainly fit into the family in that way, although he is also effectively a stranger, one who has been cruel and destructive, which raises the second irony. Like the men before him, the Doctor is only misleading Blanche for the moment, to suit his purpose. Once he has her at the hospital, she will be forgotten as Blanche has been forgotten by the men with whom she has slept over the years.

The two walk through the kitchen where the poker players stand silently waiting for her to leave. As they walk down the porch steps, Stella cries out three times, her sister's name. Blanche gives no indication of having heard it. She is like a woman in a dream, one of narcoticized dead Williams refers to earlier in the play. With the Nurse in tow, Blanche and the Doctor turn the corner and Stella is left weeping on the stairs. To comfort her, Eunice brings the baby down and settles it in her arms, completing the juxtaposition of destruction (Blanche) and creation (the baby) (Tharpe 93). Eunice then walks into the kitchen where the men are resuming their card game as if Blanche's commitment is just another average day in the Quarter. On the stairs, Williams again returns us to an earlier moment in the play. Stella and Stanley are on the steps again and instead of animal lust, Stella gives in to a full, wild expression of sorrow as she sobs on the stairs. Stanley, uncertain of how his wife will receive him, tentatively calls out her name, then sits beside her on the stairs, murmuring words of comfort, and wriggling his fingers into her blouse, to placate her with sex. Theirs is still a marriage of sexual thraldom, although the end is ambiguous. It is not fully clear whether Stella will accept him into her bed again. Though she does not brush away his fingers, she is in a state of extreme emotion. There is no telling what will happen tomorrow.

Looking at the patterning of the play, and the placement of the poker game at both the beginning and the end of the scene, one could assume that Stanley is the victor. Steve offers the last line of the play when he says, "The game is seven-card stud." telling the audience that ultimately the game is stud, it is the man's game and not the women's that will be played. Stanley Kowlaski, and his world order, of grim reality will triumph over the fragile and ethereal world of Blanche DuBois.

Works Cited

Bloom, Harold, ed. *Modern Critical Views: Tennessee Williams*. New York: Chelsea House Publications, 1987.

Griffin, Alice. *Understanding Tennessee Williams*. Columbia, South Carolina: University of South Carolina Press, 1995.

Gross, Robert F., ed. *Tennessee Williams: A Casebook*. New York: Routledge, 2002.

O'Connor, Jacqueline. *Dramatizing Dementia: Madness in the Plays of Tennessee Williams*. Bowling Green, OH: Bowling Green University Popular Press, 1997.

Pagan, Nicholas. *Rethinking Literary Biography: A Postmodern Approach to Tennessee Williams*. Rutherford: Farleigh Dickinson University Press, 1993.

Roudane, Matthew C., ed. *The Cambridge Companion to Tennessee Williams*. Cambridge: Cambridge University Press, 1997.

Stanton, Stephen S., ed. *Tennessee Williams: A Collection of Critical Essays*. Englewood Cliffs, NJ: Prentice Hall, Inc., 1977.

Tharpe, Jac, ed. *Tennessee Williams: A Tribute.* Jackson: University Press of Mississippi, 1977.

Voss, Ralph F., ed. *Magical Muse: Millennial Essays on Tennessee Williams.* Tuscaloosa: University of Alabama Press, 2002.

Critical Views

I begin with Desire, the play's largest idea. Literally, Desire is a streetcar on which Blanche rides until she transfers to a streetcar named Cemeteries in order to arrive in Elysian Fields, where Stella and Stanley live. The symbolic names are characteristic of the dramatic art of Tennessee Williams, for whom symbols are the "natural speech of drama." Their import is obvious. Blanche, in her painful past, has experienced desire and death, and now is entering a "paradise" where she will be considered an intruder and from which she will be expelled. But Desire is a streetcar on which Stanley also rides for in the specific vocabulary of the play Desire means sexual desires. When Blanche tells Mitch the opposite of death is desire, she goes on to say that she answered the calls of the young soldiers who, when drunk, called her name on her lawn, and she went out to sleep with them. A former soldier, Stanley, also drunk, answering the call within him, rapes her. Sex is the play's great leveller. The genteel Blanche and the raw Stanley ride the same streetcar, but for different reasons. Blanche goes to her sexual affairs to relieve the broken quality of her life, looking for closeness, perhaps kindness, in that physical way. She cannot see herself as a whore because sexual activity was for her a temporary means for needed affection, the only refuge for her lonely soul. Stanley rides the streetcar because that is the necessary physical function of his life, natural, never compensating for emotional agony because his soul is never lost, what Blanche calls "brutal desire—just—Desire!" Desire is the common ground on which Stan and Blanche meet, a streetcar on which both are passengers, the scales on which both are measured. On one side of the scale a fading, fragile woman for whom sexual activity is a temporary release from loneliness; on the other side a crude, physical man for whom sexual activity is a normal function of life. The needs of both are clearly presented by Williams and should be clearly understood by the audience, which must neither wholly condemn Blanche for her whorishness nor Stanley for his brutishness. The scales are balanced so finely that when Stanley condemns Blanche for her sexual looseness and Blanche condemns Stanley for his apishness, each seems *both* right and wrong, right in the light of truth, wrong in the light of understanding.

Desire or sexual impulse, therefore, is common to both Blanche and Stanley and provides one measure of their similarity and difference. They share other measures as well. They compete for the possession of Stella, for the affections of Mitch; they share the bottle of whisky; they dress and undress in the view of others; they both wish to occupy the bathroom. The first and the last deserve brief comment.

Stella shares Blanche's past and Stanley's present. Having a memory of Belle Reve, Stella, according to Blanche, surely cannot live in this place with that beast. Blanche, who allowed sexual affairs to fill her emotional need, cannot understand her sister's need for sexual activity with Stanley. In scene three Blanche physically takes Stella away from Stanley, guiding her upstairs after Stella is beaten by Stanley. But Stella's return down those stairs, when Stanley calls her at the end of the same scene, demonstrates her allegiance to him. Her euphoric state the next morning, after a night of pleasurable lovemaking, seals her bonded fate. Blanche appeals to Stella with tenderness and with arguments about the past and civilization, touching the heart and mind; Stanley touches the body. For Stella, "the things that happen between a man and a woman in the dark" make everything else unimportant.

The bathroom, realistic and unseen, provides an interesting setting for the dialectic of character, with Blanche and Stanley again in opposition, with the bathroom itself a battleground. Blanche needs her bath to calm her nerves, she says. She bathes and bathes, the steaming hot water washing her body but never penetrating to cleanse her soul. The hot water and soap cannot make clean a sordid past, and her perfumes cannot sweeten her tainted mortality. The ritual of the bath is useless; she must ever return to it because, like her sexual activity, it provides only temporary relief. Final relief for Blanche will come only with her death, and she will die, she claims, "on the sea." The difference between the bath water in Stanley's bathroom and the "ocean as blue as my lovers eyes" is the distance between Blanche's hellish present and her image of a heavenly death. Whereas Blanche needs the bathroom to relieve her nerves, Stanley needs it to relieve his kidneys. The room is one, but the activity is two: for Blanche a bath, for Stanley a toilet. A dialectic between claims in a metaphorical setting.

Light, one of the play's important symbols, provides a wide range of reference, but always reveals Williams' complementary vision. Most fiercely bright is the bulb with a vivid green glass shade which hangs over the poker table. It shines down on men "at the peak of their physical manhood" playing poker. Its glare is the vivid glare of reality. So too is the bulb over Blanche's bed before she puts a paper lantern over it. That she must cover the light and live in the shadow indicates her twilight condition and her attitude toward life: "I don't want realism. I want magic!" Blanche lives between light and dark, avoiding the truthful glare of the former and unable to find the latter. Stanley, on the other hand, can live in light *and* dark. Realism is what he wants, and the world he occupies, *his* world, displays primary colors. But when he wants the dark— for the things that happen between a man and a woman—he can break the bulbs, as he did on his wedding night. Stanley functions in both light and dark; Blanche, delicate as a moth, must avoid strong light. Stanley, himself a garish sun, claims Stella, the star. Blanche neither generates light nor reflects light. She can only sing in her bath about a paper moon in a make-believe world. Paper moon, paper lantern, paper boy collecting money for *The Evening Star*—all manifestations of Blanche's gossamer grip on reality. The light of a bulb, a moon, a star, offering both standard and unique associations, are manipulated by Williams to extend his relentless dialectic.

FRANK BRADLEY ON THE METAPHORS OF SPACE

As the title suggests, *Streetcar* embraces the metaphor of movement, or more specifically, public transit, in order to engage the question of dramatic *vérité* in a world in which private relations have become problematic. The companionship which Blanche seeks must find a means of expression and enactment in a stage environment which has shaken the home's foundation and thereby blurred distinctions between private and public.

Although the home in *Streetcar*—the Kowalski apartment—still stands, it does so largely in the character of an environmental antagonist to Blanche. Her chief problem in the dirty, crowded, and oppressive apartment is that she is subject to too many personal disclosures at the hands of too many strangers, and on terms not her own. The apartment crowds a number of people into a very small space, and is itself surrounded by other spaces of intrusive activity which condition it. The location of the Hubbel apartment upstairs, the flimsiness of walls, and the necessity of open windows to combat the New Orleans heat and humidity guarantee that the Kowalskis and the Hubbels will never be free from each other. As if this weren't enough, Williams adds the device of making the back wall of the apartment transparent at times so that we might be reminded of the conditioning of the action within by a larger outside context, as he describes during the scene which immediately precedes the inevitable "date" that Blanche and Stanley have "had with each other since the beginning":

> *Through the back wall of the rooms, which have become transparent, can be seen the sidewalk. A prostitute has rolled a drunkard. He pursues her along the walk, overtakes her and there is a struggle. A policeman's whistle breaks it up. The figures disappear.* (399)

Voices and sounds from the outside keep intruding on attempted "private" dialogues: Blanche asks Stella if she may "speak—*plainly*" her opinions of Stanley's brutishness, at which point the loud sound of a train approaching temporarily makes hearing her impossible (322).

Inside the apartment there are no doors between rooms, and there are only two rooms. Its inhabitants must undress in view of each other. Nothing is safe from another person's scrutiny in such a space. It is significant that Stanley's first penetration of Blanche's privacy happens largely as a result of space and proximity: because there is literally no place for Blanche's trunk to be stored, it must remain throughout the play in a high-traffic area in Stanley and Stella's bedroom, vulnerable to Stanley's rough dissection as he hurls about the room the remaining vestiges of her private life—her dresses, furs, jewelry, and love letters (273–274). That Blanche's bed is in the most public place of all—a kitchen, where Stanley and his friends play poker—serves as a constant reminder of her all-too-public past while at the same time it visually reinforces the problem of her present lack of privacy. To lack privacy is to be exposed to multiple and often conflicting outside influences. To be public is to be impure, and every space in this setting is impure. Even the home's most private space, the bathroom, does uncomfortable double duty: Blanche's periodic rejuvenating baths occur in the same space where Stanley and his friends urinate.

As was the case in Diderot's time, the domicile in Williams's world reinforces the value system of its paterfamilias. Stanley's explanation of the Napoleonic code suggests that everything in the apartment bears his mark. By this principle alone he appears far better accommodated to living in crowded conditions which blur the distinction between private and public. He is a man of the present, well-adjusted to an instrumental world which has no time for Blanche's ornate literary discourse, but insists on laying his cards on the table (279). But if the environment of Elysian Fields antagonizes Blanche, her mere presence antagonizes Stanley. He feels the pressure of having his space violated by a stranger, as he complains to Stella:

God, honey, it's gonna be sweet when we can make noise

in the night the way that we used to and get the colored lights going with nobody's sister behind the curtains to hear us! (373)

To lack privacy in this broken home is to lack the ability to speak purely (even if, in Stanley's case, speaking purely means nothing more than making noise), to disclose oneself with completeness and sincerity, and on one's own terms. Speech is inevitably compromised in this instrumental space; the search for *vérité*, the "sincere kindly voices with the ring of truth," takes place on grounds that make its achievement virtually impossible to enact.

Compromised language, no longer capable of manifesting the intersubjective bond that Blanche desires, becomes in *Streetcar* as menacing and disorienting as the alien environment in which she wanders. A literary figure (she was an English teacher) set loose in a brutal and instrumental world, Blanche bears witness to a trail of broken meanings which intensify her fragmentation. Her arrival at the Kowalski apartment in the opening scene betrays a naïve faith in words to mean what they say in a crude world governed by insincere relations. She stands bewildered that the reality of her destination, Elysian Fields, contradicts the literary image of paradise that she had heretofore accepted; she uncomprehendingly mutters to the stranger Eunice that "[t]hey mustn't have—understood—what number I wanted" (246). As one who spent a teaching career trying to "instill a bunch of bobby-soxers and drugstore Romeos with a reverence for Hawthorne and Whitman and Poe" (302), Blanche relies upon the literary reference in order to help stabilize her in disorienting surroundings, as she describes her reaction to Elysian Fields to Stella:

Never, never, never in my worst dreams could I picture— Only Poe! Only Mr. Edgar Allan Poe!—could do it justice! Out there I suppose is the ghoul-haunted woodland of Weir! (20)

Yet as much as Blanche relies upon the literary reference to give orientation, such reference has itself become degraded in her world. Her life in Laurel was characterized by linguistic disjunctions, between the name of "Belle Reve" and its "epic fornications" and "long parade to the graveyard," between "English Teacher" and "spinster," "Flamingo" and "Tarantula Arms," "Sister Blanche" and "Dame Blanche, "lover" and "degenerate," to name but a few. Little wonder then, that the object of her search is a cessation of what has become a long journey of dislocations. A "restful" bond with Mitch, who carries with him as a memento of a former romance a cigarette case with Blanche's "favorite sonnet by Mrs. Browning" might, in Blanche's mind, resurrect the power of language to keep an unstable, possessive, and libidinous world at bay, as it no doubt would have in Diderot's day (297). But Blanche's past, which buried the private identity she seeks to restore, that of the daughter of the family more "tender and trusting" than anyone, under the public mask of a profligate, becomes a means by which Stanley can banish what he perceives as her ornate pretensions and return to his household its pure language, a language of ecstatic shrieks and violent shouts, a language to which his wife, unlike her sister, seems well accustomed.

BERT CARDULLO ON BLANCHE'S RELATIONSHIP WITH STELLA

As I have observed, those critics of *Streetcar* who dismiss the play outright as tragedy point to the character of Blanche as indisputably that of a clinical case history; they claim that the collapse of her marriage and the death of her homosexual husband made her a victim of neurosis. But they fail to take into account, in Leonard Berkman's words, that "Blanche's most fundamental regret is not that she happened to marry a homosexual," not the *discovery* of Allan's homosexuality (*Stella* believes this). It is that, "when made aware of her husband's homosexuality, she brought on [his] suicide by her unqualified expression of disgust," her *failure* to be compassionate (p. 253).

Confronted in theory with the choice between the expression of compassion and the expression of disgust at the sudden and stunning revelation of Allan's longstanding affair with an older man, she at first "pretended that nothing had been discovered" (p. 355). Then, unable to stop herself, she blurted out abruptly the words of contempt that drove her first and only love to kill himself. I say "confronted in theory with the choice" because, as Blanche herself confesses to Mitch, "[Allan] came to me for help. I didn't know that.... All I knew was I'd failed him in some mysterious way and wasn't able to give the help he needed but couldn't speak of! ... I loved him unendurably but without being able to help him or help myself" (p. 354). Blanche could hardly be expected to respond with love and understanding to her discovery, "in the worst of all possible ways," of Allan's homosexuality (though she struggles to—that is one reason she does not express her disgust immediately), because she had never had a truly intimate, an open and trusting, relationship with him. In the same way, Williams leads us to believe she had never had such a relationship with any of her relatives at Belle Reve either, nor they with one another, as the DuBois men gradually exchanged the land for their "epic fornications" and the women dared not admit they had ever heard of death.

The evidence in the present for this conclusion is her relationship with Stella—hardly what could be called one of confidence and intimacy, despite the genuine feeling the sisters have for each other. As Blanche dreams airily in act one of Shep Huntleigh's block-long Cadillac convertible and a shop for *both* of them, Stella straightens up her apartment matter of factly and responds to her sister practically, if lightly, even disinterestedly. When Blanche cries out in desperation that she has left only "sixty-five measly cents in coin of the realm," Stella answers this veiled plea for rescue from a life bereft of warmth and affection with little more than an offer of five dollars and a Bromo and the suggestion that she "just let things go, at least for a—while" (p. 319). Stella, out of an overwhelming desire to negate her past and Blanche with it, or out of sheer self-indulgence, will, *can*, concern herself with nothing but the mindless and easy, sensuous pursuit of day-to-day living. When Blanche opens up to her in act two and speaks of "soft people" and "fading," Stella can only reject what she calls morbidity and offer her sister a Coke, even as she offered to pour the drinks in act one, scene one. And when at the end of act three, scene one, Blanche wants to know what has happened, Stella is unable to confront her with what Stanley has reported, even as Blanche herself was unable to confront Allan with what she had discovered until it was too late. In a stunning unmasking of character toward the end of the same scene, Stella reacts to Stanley's purchase of the bus ticket with, "In the first place, Blanche wouldn't go on a bus" (p. 367). She objects to the *means* of transportation instead of expressing immediate incredulity, outrage, and dismay at the *idea* of sending her sister away.

Blanche is closer to tragic heroine than many would like to think, then, "in [her] refusal to shirk a responsibility that the conventional society of her time and place would have eagerly excused ...," to quote Leonard Berkman (p. 253). She refuses from the beginning to forgive herself for denying Allan the compassion that would have saved and perhaps changed him, or at any rate made his burden easier to bear. She struggles at the end in his memory to achieve intimacy with Mitch—the only true intimacy within her grasp—which alone can restore her to grace through its inherent linking of sex with compassion. It is thus not arbitrarily or gratuitously, or simply out of her own pure joy, that Williams has Blanche declare, "Sometimes—there's God—so quickly!" at the end of act two, scene two (p. 356). Rather, he has her so re-enter a state of grace as a direct result of the embrace and kiss she exchanges with Mitch,[3] of their recognition, finally, of a real need and desire for one another. In this light, the "intimacies with strangers," the sex *without* compassion, she turned to after her husband's suicide come to appear less the free-standing acts of a nymphomaniac than those of a woman trying to find momentary relief or "protection" without having deeply personal demands placed on her. Blanche sought to "fill [her] empty heart" at the same time that she reaffirmed a sexuality lost on Allan's attraction to men and "denied" the death of so many of her relatives. As Stanley himself says, "They [the 'strangers'] got wised up after two or three dates with her and then they quit, and she goes on to another, the same old line, same old act, same old hooey!" (p. 361). This suggests that these "strangers," in "wising up" to Blanche's thinly disguised cries for help and devotion as well as to the artifice and affectation of her ways, were as much to blame for her panic-driven promiscuity as she herself was.

To be sure, the nobility and grandeur of Blanche's character are marred by her intemperance, be it manifested through her passion for drink, her appetite for sex, or her intolerance of Stanley's lifestyle (all of which she strives with varying degrees of willpower, and success, to overcome). But it is not this flaw which brings about her downfall. Neither is it her predisposition to gloss over the harsh realities of life by pretending that they are simply not there, as is popularly believed. (This "flaw" is responsible for her very survival as much as it is for her adversity.) In any case, it is not flaws which precipitate the downfall of great tragic characters. "Truly dramatic flaws," notes Bert O. States in *Irony and Drama*, "are such as ... to make [tragic heroes] ambiguously fallible," are what "rescues [them] from perfection in the process of being doomed" (pp. 53–54). Blanche DuBois may fall short of traditional greatness as tragic heroine, but doomed she is from the first by the "very different circumstances" under which she grew up and against which she struggled long after Stella had fled to New Orleans. The absence of truth and intimacy from life at Belle Reve is what drove Blanche into an early marriage and on the road to calamity, as is the stagnancy, the decadence, of postbellum plantation life what prompted her sister to opt for the vitality of New Orleans and marriage to a man whose virility could never be questioned. Thus, Blanche's clash with Stanley, specifically, her condemnation of him to Stella at the end of act one, scene four, cannot be construed as the sole, absolute cause of her downfall, without whose occurrence, say, her troubles would eventually have vanished or before which they could scarcely be said to have been pressing. On the contrary, such clash must be viewed as the *result* of her attempt to achieve an intimacy with Stella which had never before existed between them. It is an inevitable *addition* to a long line of unfortunate incidents stemming from the failure of communion over many years to pervade the lives of the DuBois men and women. Blanche does not criticize Stanley the morning after "The Poker Night" simply for the sake of criticizing him, of extolling the virtues of life at Belle Reve at his expense. Her harangue is designed, above all else, to draw her closer to her sister, to unite them in "light" and "progress" against "barbarianism." Blanche wishes to "get out" and "make a new life" at this point, not so much because she fears Stanley will destroy her as because she deplores his way of life, whose corrupting influence, she feels, prevents her from attaining intimacy with Stella. Departing Stanley's company alone will do her no good, and she knows it. Her sprightly attraction to him in act one, scene two, in spite of his coarseness, tells us she has probably run into his general type in the past, and we are well aware that her flight from Laurel and the assorted "types" of the Hotel Flamingo, among other spots, has done little to alleviate her distress. Escaping Stanley in the company of Stella will lead, she hopes, to the solidification of a bond between them; to their increased compassion for each other's lot, and consequently to a new life some place where the past might at least be brought fully to light, if not somehow atoned for.

Note
3. Berkman, p. 254.

RUBY COHN ON MODES OF CHARACTERIZATION

To play her role in the two-room Kowalski apartment, Blanche has brought a trunk full of clothes; her stage business involves drinking, dimming lights, emerging from hot baths, and seeking compliments about her appearance. But it is mainly through her dialogue that Blanche underlines her manor-born superiority. She introduces cultural references into the French Quarter dwelling, which evokes an Edgar Allen Poe horror story for her. She recognizes that the lines on Mitch's cigarette case belong to a sonnet by Mrs. Browning; she has evidently taught American literature, since she mentions Poe, Hawthorne, and Whitman. She calls the newspaper boy a young Prince out of the Arabian nights, and Mitch her Rosenkavalier, Armand, and Samson. In the last scene, Blanche is blind to the reality of her situation, but she specifies that her jacket is Della Robbia blue: "the blue of the robe in the old Madonna pictures."

Blanche's speech is distinguished not only by her cultural references. She alone uses correct grammar and varied syntax. Her vocabulary contains such Latinisms as "heterogeneous," "absconding," "judicial," "transitory," and "recriminations." But when Blanche uses images, they are stale or incongruous. Defeated, she tells Mitch that she had viewed him as "a cleft in the rock of the world that I could hide in." A little later, she compares her past to "an old tin can [on] the tail of the kite." Of her soldier boy-friends, Blanche remarks: "The paddy-wagon would gather them up like daisies." Even her most moving speech—the story of her husband's suicide—closes with pretentious imagery: "And then the searchlight which had been turned on the world was turned off again and never for one moment since has there been any light that's stronger than this—kitchen—candle." Seemingly related but not functionally linked is her hope that Stella's baby will have eyes "like two blue candles lighted in a white cake."

When Blanche tries to be uplifting, her images are most inadequate. Seeking to inspire Stella, she becomes trite and abstract: poetry and music, new light, tender feelings, our flag. When Blanche insists upon her superiority to Stanley, she can summon only the cliché phrases of popular magazines: "But beauty of the mind and richness of the spirit and tenderness of the heart—and I have all of those things—aren't taken away, but grow!" Whatever Williams may have intended, Blanche

DuBois is trapped by the poverty of her imagery which reflects the poverty of her dreams, like Miller's Willy Loman. But whereas Miller supplies Willy with weak foils, Blanche is challenged and destroyed by a strong antagonist, Stanley Kowalski, whom she correctly views as her executioner. The hard consonants of Stanley Kowalski contrast with the open vowels of Blanche DuBois. As opposed to her mothlike whiteness, Stanley moves in a world of vivid color; Williams compares him to "*a richly feathered male bird.*" Stanley wears a green bowling shirt or bright silk pajamas. He and Stella make love under colored lights. His poker party resembles Van Gogh's *Night Cafe*, with its "*raw colors of childhood's spectrum.*" Visually and verbally, Williams' opposes Stanley to Blanche. Each character is summarized by his opening lines:

Stanley. Hey, there! Stella, Baby!.... Catch! ... Meat!
Blanche. They told me to take a streetcar named Desire, and then transfer to one called Cemeteries and ride six blocks and get off at—Elysian Fields!

Stanley has trained his wife to catch his meat, in every sense. Blanche has come to the end of the line named Desire, and Williams' drama traces her ride to Cemeteries. Forcing her toward that destination is the implacable solidity of Stanley's speech: "Be comfortable is my motto." "You going to shack up here?" "To hold front position in this rat-race you've got to believe you are lucky." "You left nothing here but spilt talcum and old empty perfume bottles—unless it's the paper lantern you want to take with you."

On stage, Stanley's physicality contrasts with Blanche's ready verbalizations. His cruellest gesture in the play is to tear the paper lantern off the light bulb. His other rough acts are understandable—tossing the meat package to Stella, ruffling Blanche's rich clothes, throwing the radio out of the window, breaking plates when he is insulted, and handing Blanche a one-way ticket to Laurel. We do not see Stanley hit Stella, and we do not see him rape Blanche; the first deed is mitigated by his contrition, and the second by Blanche's provocation. In the last scene of the play, however, when Blanche is helpless and defeated, Stanley acts with the kind of cruelty that Blanche has called "unforgivable," and of which she herself was guilty when she told her young husband: "You disgust me."

Blanche and Stanley are protagonist and antagonist in *Streetcar*, and yet, whatever Williams has said in commentary, his play is not a simple picture of victim and villain. Blanche is cruel to her husband, rude to Eunice, patronizing to Stella, and arrogant to Stanley. Though Stanley is finally cruel to Blanche, he is a faithful friend to Mitch and a satisfying husband to Stella. Especially as played by Marlon Brando, Stanley hides vulnerability beneath taunts and boasts; his cruelty defends his world.

Between Blanche and Stanley are Stella and Mitch, each part-victim and part-brute. Naturally kind, admittedly sensual, Stella is ironically named for a star. She remembers Belle Reve without nostalgia, and she lives contentedly in the Elysian Fields, acquiescing to Stanley's dominance as quietly as she evidently did to Blanche in their childhood. "Thrilled" by Stanley, she accepts all facets of his violence—except the truth of his rape of her sister.

Like Stella, Mitch is pulled between Stanley and Blanche. Responsive to women, Mitch willingly accedes to Blanche's instructions in gentility, and he suffers visibly at Stanley's revelations about her past. An Army buddy, fellow-worker, and poker pal of Stanley, Mitch shares Stanley's ethics—"Poker should not be played in a house with women." But he also shares Blanche's awareness of death. Mitch has a dead girl-friend as Blanche has a dead husband. As Blanche watched the members of her family die, Mitch is watching his mother die. Mitch's feeling for his dying mother elicits Blanche's confession of her husband's suicide. Death makes them realize their need of one another. But after Mitch learns about Blanche's past, a Mexican woman chants: "Flores. Flores. Flores para los muertos." It is not clear whether Blanche understands the Spanish, but she reminisces on the same theme: "Death—I used to sit here and she used to sit over there and death was as close as you are." Death of the mind is as close to Blanche as

Mitch is. By the next scene, even before the rape, Blanche panics into derangement.

The play's last scene so victimizes Blanche—sister, brother-in-law, poker players, nurse—that it borders on sentimentality, which is aggravated, in reading, by such pretentious stage directions as "*tragic radiance*" for Blanche, on whose face "*all human experience shows.*" But Williams saves the scene by the very triviality of the dialogue—Blanche's preoccupation with her adornments, the men's preoccupation with their poker game. Both preoccupations have been repeated during the course of the play, so that they take on cumulative significance in this last scene. Other repeated motifs culminate in this scene—the Shep Huntleigh of Blanche's fantasy, her hot bath and search for compliments, her references to death, the distortion of the "Varsouviana" into jungle noises, Stanley's revelation of the naked light bulb. At the last, Blanche follows the doctor as blindly as she followed Stella during the first poker game. Once Blanche is gone, civilized discourse vanishes, Stanley and Stella relax into an almost wordless animal abandon as we hear the blue piano music and the final words of the play: "This game is seven-card stud," which summarizes life in the French Quarter.

MARY ANN CORRIGAN ON ILLUSION AND REALITY

Blanche, although revelling in her fantasies, is still capable of distinguishing them from actual events. In the middle of her feigned discussion with her admirers she catches sight of her face in a hand mirror, recognizes it as real, and breaks the mirror. At this point Stanley appears in his "*vivid green silk bowling shirt,*" to the tune of honky-tonk music, which continues to be heard throughout the scene. When Stanley confronts Blanche with his knowledge of her background, the abominable reality that Blanche detests begins to impinge upon her: "*Lurid reflections appear on the walls around Blanche. The shadows are of a grotesque and menacing form. She catches her breath, crosses to the phone and jiggles the hook.*" For Blanche the telephone is an avenue to a better world. When she sought what she called a "way out" for herself and Stella in Scene III, the telephone and telegraph were the means to effect her plan. Again she attempts to escape into a different world by calling her Texas millionaire. But when she can't give a number or an address, the operator cuts her off. Reality again! The stage directions indicate the result on Blanche of this thwarting of her plans: "*She sets the phone down and crosses warily into the kitchen. The night is filled with inhuman voices like cries in a jungle.*" Blanche has been sensitive to sound throughout the play. In the first act she jumped at the screech of a cat; later, when Stanley slammed a drawer closed, she winced in pain. Now "the cacophony that we hear is inside Blanche's head— imaginary sounds and real sounds turned grotesque and horrible by her fear."[5] To make Blanche's mounting fears tangible Williams uses the scrim:

> *Through the back wall of the rooms, which have become transparent, can be seen the sidewalk. A prostitute has rolled a drunkard. He pursues her along the walk, overtakes her and there is a struggle. A policeman's whistle breaks it up. The figures disappear. Some moments later the Negro woman appears around the corner with a sequined bag which the prostitute had dropped on the walk. She is rooting excitedly through it.*

The New Orleans street figures are analogues of all that reality means to Blanche: violence, theft, immorality, bestiality. No wonder she tries to escape it. She returns to the telephone: "Western Union? Yes! I—want to—Take down this message! 'In desperate, desperate circumstances! Help me! Caught in a trap. Caught in—' Oh!" There is no escaping reality now, for its arch crusader, Stanley, is back:

> *The bathroom door is thrown open and Stanley comes out in the brilliant silk pajamas. He grins at her as he knots the tattled sash about his waist.... The barely audible 'blue piano' begins to*

drum up louder. The sound of it turns into the roar of an approaching locomotive....

Blanche reads the meaning of the sounds perfectly: she will be forced to become part of this world of hot music and lust. Her tormentor teases her with the spectre of her fears:

You think I'll interfere with you? Ha-ha!
(*The 'blue piano' goes softly. She turns confusedly and makes a faint gesture. The inhuman jungle voices rise up. He takes a step toward her, biting his tongue which protrudes between his lips.*)

Blanche's gesture of threatening Stanley with a broken bottle is the last and the easiest of the challenges she poses for him. Springing like an animal at prey, he catches her. wrist: "*The bottle top falls. She sinks to her knees. He picks up her inert figure and carries her to the bed. The hot trumpet and drums from the Four Deuces sound loudly.*" Blanche's involuntary journey to the depths of sordidness results in her losing contact completely with any kind of reality. The theatrical devices, aural and visual, which represent not objective occurrence, but inner action, enable the audience to understand Blanche's ordeal and her retreat into insanity.

Williams depicts the total defeat of a woman whose existence depends on her maintaining illusions about herself and the world. Blanche is both a representative and a victim of a tradition that taught her that attractiveness, virtue, and gentility led automatically to happiness. But reality proved intractable to the myth. Blanche's lot was Belle Reve, with its debts and deaths, and a homosexual husband who killed himself because, for once, her sensitivity failed her. Blanche's "amatory adventures ... are the unwholesome means she uses to maintain her connection with life, to fight the sense of death which her whole background has created in her."[6] Since "the tradition" allows no place for the physical and sensual, she rejects this aspect of her personality, calling it "brutal desire." Kazan writes: "She thinks she sins when she gives into it ... yet she does give into it, out of loneliness ... but by calling it 'brutal desire,' she is able to separate it from her 'real self,' her 'cultured,' refined self."[7]

If Blanche is the last remnant of a moribund culture, Stanley is in the vanguard of a vital and different society. Even Blanche recognizes his strength when she says, "He's just not the type that goes for jasmine perfume, but maybe he's what we need to mix with our blood now that we've lost Belle Reve" (Scene II). If Blanche's philosophy cannot make room for "brutal desire," Stanley's comprehends little else. Williams describes him:

> *Since earliest manhood the center of his life has been pleasure with women.... He sizes women up at a glance, with sexual classifications, crude images flashing into his mind and determining the way he smiles at them.* (Scene I)

It is only fitting that Stanley destroy Blanche with sex. As Benjamin Nelson writes, sex "has been her Achilles heel. It has always been his sword and shield."[8]

The conflict between Blanche and Stanley is an externalization of the conflict that goes on within Blanche between illusion and reality. The illusion sustaining her is her image of herself as a Southern belle, a fine, cultured, young lady. The reality is a lonely woman, desperately seeking human contact, indulging "brutal desire" as an affirmation of life. Blanche's "schizoid personality is a drama of man's irreconcilable split between animal reality and moral appearance."[9] This drama is played out not only in Blanche's mind, but between Stanley and Blanche as well. Stanley strips away Blanche's illusions and forces her to face animal reality. In doing so, he demonstrates that reality is as brutal as she feared She has no choice but to retreat totally into illusion. Thus, the external events of the play, while actually occurring, serve as a metaphor for Blanche's internal conflict.

In pitting Blanche and Stanley against one another, Williams returns to his oft-told tale of the defeat of the weak by the strong. But, for a change, both figures represent complex and morally ambiguous positions. Blanche is far from perfect. She is a liar, an alcoholic, and she would break up the Kowalski marriage if she could. Despite his rough exterior, Stanley genuinely loves and needs his wife, and he cannot be blamed for protecting his marriage against the force that would destroy it. The ambiguity of Blanche and Stanley makes them more realistic than many of Williams' characters, who are often either demons (philistines with power, wealth and influence) or angels (helpless, sensitive, downtrodden artists or women). Although Williams depicts both positive and negative personality traits in Blanche and Stanley, his attitude toward the two characters changes in the course of the play. In the beginning Williams clearly favors Stanley by emphasizing his wholesome natural traits, while dwelling on Blanche's artificiality. But such, we learn, are the deceptive appearances. The more Williams delves into Blanche's inner life and presents it on stage, the more sympathetic she becomes. Stanley's true nature also becomes apparent, in its negative effect upon her psyche, and, in the end, she is the undisputed moral victor.

Kazan's production deliberately emphasized Stanley's positive traits. In his notes on directing the play Kazan specifies that Blanche be presented as the "heavy" at the beginning of the play. Simultaneously, of course, Stanley is to evoke the audience's sympathy. Harold Clurman reports on this aspect of the original production: "Because the author does not preach about him but draws him without hate or ideological animus, the audience takes him at his face value.... For almost more than two-thirds of the play, therefore, the audience identifies itself with Stanley Kowalski. His low jeering is seconded by the audience's laughter, which seems to mock the feeble and hysterical decorativeness of the girl's behavior"[10] Clurman, in going on to condemn the attempt to ingratiate Stanley with the audience, overlooks the dramatic value of making Stanley appealing initially. Stanley is, after all, not a monster. He bears remarkable resemblance to the kind of hero that Americans love, the hero of the westerns or the tough detective stories: the gruff masculine pragmatist who commands the adulation of women even as he scorns them for his male companions. That he is not as harmless, as "right" as he seems is precisely Williams' point. The play forces the members of the audience, as well as Blanche, to face "harsh reality," for they learn that what they instinctively admire and view as healthy is really a base egotistical force, destructive of what it cannot comprehend. The audience too moves from illusion to reality. The initial tendency is to resent Blanche and her airs, to applaud Stanley every time he "takes her down a peg." But slowly, as the veil of illusion lifts, both Stanley and Blanche are seen more clearly. Marlon Brando, who played Stanley in the Kazan production and in the movie, was an excellent choice for an appealing Stanley. Irwin Shaw commented on Brando's Broadway performance:

He is to appealing in a direct, almost childlike way in the beginning and we have been so conditioned by the modern doctrine that what is natural is good, that we admire him and sympathize with him. Then, bit by bit, with a full account of what his good points really are, we come dimly to see that he is ... brutish, destructive in his healthy egotism, dangerous, immoral, surviving.[11]

It is the rape scene that finally reveals the true horror of Stanley. As Blanche is made to face unpleasant reality in this scene, so is the audience.[12]

Williams remains as much as possible within the conventions of verisimilitude in using theatrical devices to reveal Blanche's distorted vision of reality. The audience is, however, aware that baths and light bulbs have a meaning for Blanche apart from their functional existence. The further Blanche retreats from reality, the more Williams distorts the surface realism of the play. The purpose of the transparent wall in Scene I is not to reveal what is actually occurring in the alley, but to provide the necessary milieu for the defeat of illusion and to offer objective correlatives for Blanche's fears. Similarly, the subjective sounds enable the audience to share Blanche's past experiences and her present terrors.

Notes

5. Weales, p. 106.

6. Harold Clurman, *The Divine Pastime* (New York, 1974), p. 12.

7. Kazan, p. 368.

8. Benjamin Nelson, *Tennessee Williams: The Man and His Work* (New York, 1961), p. 146.

9. Riddel, 425.

10. Clurman, p.16.

11. Irwin Shaw, "Masterpiece," *The New Republic*, 22 December 1947, 35.

12. The Sympathetic bond between the audience and Stanley is not merely the result of Brando's interpretation of the character. Stanley has been played differently, notably by Anthony Quinn, who emphasized the brutality of the character. But even Eric Bentley, who preferred Quinn's performance to Brando's, remarks on the inconsistency that occasionally arose between the text and the interpretation by Quinn (e.g., "When Anthony Quinn portrays Kowalski as an illiterate we are surprised at some of the big words he uses"). He also concedes: "In all fairness, I should admit that when I directed the play myself I could not stop the audience's laughing *with* Kowalski *against* Blanche." *In Search of Theater* (New York, 1947), p. 88.

ARTHUR GANZ ON PUNISHMENT AND MORALITY

The stage action of *A Streetcar Named Desire*, still Williams' finest play, consists almost entirely of the punishment that its heroine, Blanche DuBois, endures as atonement for her act of rejection, her sin in terms of Williams' morality. Since Williams begins the action of his play at a late point in the story, the act itself is not played out on stage but only referred to. Not realizing that she is describing the crime that condemns her, Blanche tells Mitch of her discovery that her adored young husband was a homosexual and of the consequences of her disgust and revulsion:

> *Blanche*.... He'd stuck the revolver into his mouth, and fired—so that the back of his head had been—blown

away! (*She sways and covers her face.*) It was because—on the dance floor—unable to stop myself—I'd suddenly said—"I saw! I know! You disgust me...." And then the searchlight which had been turned on the world was turned off again and never for one moment since has there been any light that's stronger than this— kitchen—candle....

While Blanche delivers this speech and the ones surrounding it, the polka to which she and her husband had danced, the Varsouviana, sounds in the background. At the end of the play, when Blanche sees the doctor who is to lead her off to the asylum, her punishment is complete and the Varsouviana sounds again, linking her crime to its retribution. As Blanche flees from the doctor, "the Varsouviana is filtered into a weird distortion accompanied by the cries and noises of the jungle." These symbolize simultaneously Blanche's chaotic state and the instrument of her destruction, Stanley Kowalski, the complete sensual animal, the equivalent in function to the black masseur.

Although Kowalski's primary function, to destroy Blanche, is clear, there are certain ambiguities evoked by this role. By becoming Blanche's destroyer, Kowalski also becomes the avenger of her homosexual husband. Although he is Williams' exaggeration of the Lawrencian lover, it is appropriate from Williams' point of view that Kowalski should to some degree be identified with the lonely homosexual who had been driven to suicide, for Williams saw Lawrence not only as the propagandist of sexual vitality but as the symbol of the solitary, rejected exile. (In the poem "Cried the Fox" from Williams' collection, *In the Winter of Cities*, Lawrence is seen as the fox pursued by the cruel hounds.) But however gratifying it may be to identify the embodiment of admired male sexuality with the exiled artist and thus by implication with the exiled homosexual, the identification must remain tenuous.

Kowalski, though an avenger, is as guilty of destroying Blanche as she is of destroying her husband. For Blanche, who has lost the plantation Belle Reve, the beautiful dream of a life of gracious gentility, is an exile like the homosexual; her tormentor, the ape-like Kowalski, from one point of view the representative of Lawrencian vitality, is from another the brutal, male torturer of a lonely spirit. However compassionately Blanche is viewed, she nevertheless remains a woman who, in effect, has killed her husband by her cruelty, and her attempts to turn away from death to its opposite—"the opposite is desire," as Blanche herself says—are fruitless. Even as she tells Mitch about her promiscuity, a Mexican woman stands at one side of the stage selling flowers for the dead. "*Flores para los muertos*," she calls, "*flores-flores*."

ALICE GRIFFIN ON THE SYMBOLS OF LIGHT AND WATER

In his foreword to *Camino Real* Williams states that "a symbol in a play has only one legitimate purpose, which is to say a thing more directly and simply and beautifully than it could be said in words." In *Streetcar* verbal, visual, and technical (sound and light) symbolism combine to achieve poetic drama," to use Williams's term for his plays. Light is one of the most prevalent symbols. Stanley's sole original metaphor is "colored lights" for the sex he and Stella enjoy. Blanche's "light" images are related to Allan, her first and only love: "It was like you suddenly turned a blinding light on something that had always been half in shadow." After he kills himself, "then the searchlight which had been turned on the world was turned off again and never for one moment since has there been any light that's stronger than this—kitchen—candle" (sc. 6). The light of birthday candles, usually associated with celebration, is the central metaphor of Blanche's lament in scene 8: "candles aren't safe ... candles burn out in little boys' and girls' eyes, or wind blows them out and after that happens, electric light bulbs go on and you see too plainly." Candles also suggest the attraction of the flame for "moth"—like Blanche. As the action builds, the symbol of fire (for passion) is introduced, first in Blanche's cries of "Fire!" in scene 9 and again just before the rape, Stanley's symbol of "colored lights" turns into the "shadows and lurid reflections [which] move sinuously as flames along the wall spaces."

Blanche's constant bathing suggests the traditional association of water with purification; there is also the implication of Lethe and forgetfulness. In her final aria in the last scene, beautifully lyric in its assonance, alliteration, and onomatopoeia, she says she will die on the sea "of eating an unwashed grape" and be "sewn up in a clean white sack and dropped overboard ... into an ocean as blue as my first lover's eyes!"

Among Williams's unpublished papers is a 1943 melodramatic verse play called *The Spinning Song*, which originally may have been the "Southern epic" suggested to and rejected by MGM, when he worked for them that year. In his introductory note Williams says that the play, "the story of the disintegration of a land-owning Southern family," had its origins in his seeing Eisenstein's film classic *Alexander Nevsky*:

> Its pictorial drama and poetry of atmosphere ... made me wonder if it were not possible to achieve something analogous to this in a poetic drama for the stage.... I determined to think in more plastic or visual terms. To write sparingly but with complete lyricism, and to build the play in a series of dramatic pictures. No play written in such creative terms could be naturalistic.... It would have to be a ... tragedy purified by poetry and music.[11]

In another forerunner of *Streetcar*, an unpublished one-act called *Interior: Panic*, Williams calls for "irregularities of design," including "lurid projections" on "white plaster walls," to symbolize "the hysteria" of the Blanche character.[12]

The Freudian symbolism of *Streetcar*, as well as the dialogue, action, and characterization, anticipates the rape of Blanche. Mitch's gesture of "rooting" for the key in Blanche's handbag in scene 6 is repeated in the climactic scene 10. While in the street outside the Negro Woman picks up the prostitute's handbag and "roots" through it, inside Stanley approaches Blanche. At the beginning of that scene Blanche's smashing of the hand mirror may be influenced by Cocteau's brilliant use of the image of breaking the glass of an enclosure to symbolize intercourse in his film *Beauty and the Beast*. (A breaking mirror is used as a substitute for Stanley's famous line in the film version of *Streetcar*, when Williams had to fight the Breen Office censors even to include this symbol and the implication of rape.) When in the same scene Stanley opens a bottle of beer and proffers it as a "loving-cup" to Blanche, "a geyser of foam shoots up." Then, as the blue piano becomes "the roar of an approaching locomotive" (earlier identified with Stanley as unstoppable), he "takes a step toward her, biting his tongue, which protrudes between his lips." His final gesture to Blanche in the last scene is symbolic of the rape itself, as the stage direction indicates: "Seizes the paper lantern, tearing it off the light bulb and extends it toward her. She cries out as if the lantern was herself."

The light bulb and the colored paper lantern covering it represent the contrast between the reality that Blanche cannot face and the magic she wishes to create, as she explains in scene 9: "I don't want realism.... I'll tell you what I want. Magic!" In a practical sense as well, for appearance is all-important, she wishes to shield her aging face from the "truth" of bright lights. Observes Mitch: "You never want to go out till after six and then it's always some place that's not lighted much.... I've never had a real good look at you, Blanche.... Let's turn the light on here."

Notes

11. MS., September 1943, Humanities Research Center, University of Texas at Austin. Quoted in C.W.E. Bigsby, *A Critical Introduction to Twentieth-Century American Drama* (Cambridge: Cambridge University Press, 1984), 2:56–57. Vivienne Dickson studies this and other manuscripts in the evolution of *Streetcar*, in "*A Streetcar Named Desire*: Its Development through the Manuscripts," in Tharpe, *Tennessee Williams*, 154–71.

12. MS., Humanities Research Center. Quoted in Bigsby, *Critical Introduction*, 58.

Where the mythos of tragedy leads us to look for the protagonist to articulate the value that is critical for him, we find Blanche affirming a range of values, but with a banality that gives us again, as Williams intends, the structural feature evacuated of the tragic phenomenon. "Sorrow makes for sincerity, I think," she says (p. 298). While she declares she cannot stand "a vulgar action" (p. 300), the triteness of her "favorite sonnet" and of her "attempt to instill ... reverence for Hawthorne and Whitman and Poe!"—together with her genteelness ("I brought some nice clothes to meet all your lovely friends in," "The Little Boys' Room is busy right now")—has a profound vulgarity of its own.

Although Blanche is genuinely in flight, the security sought against instinct by human self-consciousness—the security imaged for Nietzsche in the high stage, above the orchestra and the dreaming chorus—is represented in *Streetcar* as something already lost. Blanche blesses the "Seven Sisters," the Pleiades, cozily going home "all in a bunch" (p. 342). But the stars, for whom no collections need be taken up, are out of the reach of this "poor relation"; and her own sister, "Stella for star," chooses for her the ironic security of an asylum. The lofty white columns have already been "lost," and Blanche's only crown is rhinestones, "next door to glass"—assimilated, in fact, to the "Corones" for the dead (p. 388). Neither real security nor the possibility of innocence on which it depends is available to her from the beginning of the play; and therefore, despite the genuineness of her flight, the haven she describes clinks like a counterfeit: "my sister—there has been *some* progress ...! Such things as art—as poetry and music—such kinds of new light have come into the world since then! In some kinds of people some tenderer feelings have had some little beginning! ... In this dark march toward whatever it is we're approaching.... *Don't—don't hang bath with the brutes!*" (p. 323). What Blanche knows is that she must get away: hence the words she believes in are "progress," "march," "don't hang back!" The aim she posits, "such things as art—as poetry and music," is characteristic of the inevitably Apollonian tragic protagonist; but it is an aim she does not believe in. It is expressed in the clichés of the high school English class she draws upon in "improvising feverishly" to Mitch: "Physical beauty is passing. A transitory possession. But beauty of the mind and richness of the spirit and tenderness of the heart— and I have all of those things—aren't taken away, but grow! Increase with the years!" (p. 396). It should have been no surprise when these speeches, spoken by Jessica Tandy, sounded phony."[11] They serve well enough to isolate Blanche from the choral "commonness" (p. 351) of the French Quarter,[12] although they are doubtless to be associated with her "saccharine popular ballad" (p. 359)—another sample from her "heart-shaped box."

One reason she can be such a propagandist for these values at the same time she drinks heavily and takes "hydro-therapy" is that they are not the ethic she has violated, nor, in a more important way, is chastity. Obviously, she could not relieve her sense of guilt by talking all summer about the terms of it. The ethic which has been peculiarly hers, which she violated, and which, at points when she is in extremity in *Streetcar*, she obliquely reveals comes clearest where, among the eleven scenes of the play, one would expect the crisis—the sixth scene, when Blanche, drinking, on edge since Stanley mentioned Shaw, tells Mitch about her loneliness, and before that how she had fallen in love with Allan, who had come to her for help. "He was in the quicksands and clutching at me—but I wasn't holding him out, I was slipping in with him! I didn't know that. I didn't know anything except I loved him unendurably but without being able to help him or help myself. Then I found out" (p. 354). She recounts Allan's suicide, then "sways and covers her face." "It was because—," she says, "on the dance floor—unable to stop myself—I'd suddenly said—'I saw! I know! You disgust me....' And then the searchlight which had been turned on the world was turned off again and never for one moment since has there been any light that's stronger than this—kitchen—candle ..." (p. 355). Here her confession of responsibility for Allan's death is collocated exactly with the dim light in which, throughout the play, she hides herself. The years that now line her face, which is to say the cycles of guilt and flight which filled them, followed directly from her saying "I saw! I know! You disgust me." In self-loathing, she turns the sixteen-year-old girl that she was into the Tarantula, the female version of the older man in bed with Allan, repeating the act that disgusts her, then tries to escape by starting again with virginal boys.[13] Because it was she who extinguished the "blinding light," she feels every "naked bulb," now, as a merciless accusation. She tries to hide, not just her years and how she spent them, but what caused her to spend them that way. Not the deaths at Belle Reve extinguish the light, but the criminal knowledge which is death internalized.

Notes

11. See Harold Clurman, *Lies Like Truth* (New York: Macmillan, 1958), p. 79.

12. Cf. the stage direction at the beginning of scene four: "There is a confusion of street cries like a choral chant."

13. Cf. John J. Mood, "The Structure of *A Streetcar Named Desire*," *Ball State University Forum* 14: 3 (1973), 9; and R.B. Heilman, "Tennessee Williams: Approaches to Tragedy," *Southern Review* (n.s.) 1 (1965), 772.

ESTHER MERLE JACKSON ON THE ANTI-HEROIC CYCLE

In order to examine this metaphysical problem, Williams sets in motion an anti-heroic cycle of human experience. Like Dante's poet, his anti-hero traverses the downward way in his "dark night of the soul."[24] Blanche, in *A Streetcar Named Desire*, describes her descent in the spiritual cycle:

There are thousands of papers, stretching back over hundreds of years, affecting Belle Reve as, piece by piece, our improvident grandfathers and father and uncles and brothers exchanged the land for their epic fornications—to put it plainly! ... The four-letter word deprived us of our plantation, till finally all that was left—and Stella can verify that!—was the house itself and about twenty acres of ground, including a graveyard, to which now all but Stella and I have retreated. (Scene II, p. 45)

Blanche, in her downward progress toward salvation, comes to the realization of her own responsibility for suffering. She becomes aware that she suffers more for her own transgressions than for the actions of her guilty ancestors. Like Orestes, she has made a guilty choice: a choice which has involved her in the suffering of others. She suggests that she is the effective cause of her husband's death. In her moment of partial "enlightenment" she describes the critical moment when she withdrew "sympathy" from a morally helpless being:

He'd stuck the revolver into his mouth, and fired—so that the back of his head had been—blown away!
It was because—on the dance-floor—unable to stop myself—I'd suddenly said—"I saw! I know! You disgust me ..." And then the searchlight which had been turned on the world was turned off again and never for one moment since has there been any light that's stronger than this—kitchen—candle. (Scene VI, pp. 109–10)

Blanche records her descent into the hell of suffering. She describes her agony:

I, I, *I* took the blows in my face and my body! All of those deaths! The long parade to the graveyard! ... And funerals are pretty compared to deaths.... You didn't dream, but I saw! *Saw, Saw*! And now you sit there telling me with your eyes that I let the place go! How in hell do you think all that sickness and dying was paid for? Death is expensive, Miss Stella! ... (Scene I, pp. 25–26)

The play begins at a point late in the development of the anti-heroic cycle. In his record of this movement, Williams exposes Blanche's progressive fragmentation, her progress toward the last circle of hell. In *A Streetcar Named Desire*, Williams concludes his development at the ultimate point of descent; that is to say, this play closes without a clear resolution.

Note

24. The Bochum critics thought Dante to be among Williams' strongest influences, especially in *Camino Real*.

PHILIP C. KOLIN ON MITCH AS WILLIAMS' SUITOR TYPE

In *Streetcar*, Mitch also repeatedly projects an incomplete/interrupted sexuality in word and act, the hallmarks of the unsuitable suitor. Significantly, when he asks Blanche whether he may have a kiss, she responds: "Why should you be so doubtful?" Mitch's doubt, though, is a consequence of his insufficient sexuality. As Elia Kazan rightly pegged him in his *Streetcar* "Notebook," Mitch's "spine" is that of a "mama's boy," neither man nor boy, caught somewhere in between, incomplete. William Kleb wisely refers to Mitch's "arrested adolescence, even sexual confusion." Like a child, Mitch even looks sensitive, unmanly. No wonder Blanche calls him "angel puss," her most salacious epithet. Among his male friends, Mitch—the boy/man—is comically harangued for his unmanly ways; he needs a "sugar tit." He is accused of saving his poker winnings in a piggy bank for his mother. Occupationally, his sexual incompleteness is suggested by his work in the "spare parts department" at Stanley's plant. During the poker game, Mitch twice says, "Deal me out" (51, 52), separating himself from male sport. Domestically he is still caught in his mother's apron strings, metonymically represented in the Kazan film of 1951 by his leaving the washroom (Blanche's domain) still holding a towel, something literally left out that should have been left in. The incompetent wooer, Mitch is suspended between the worlds of desire and dependence, trapped in diminishment.

Mitch's language also demonstrates his sexual incompleteness—his lack of originality, psychic wholeness, integrity. He often leaves his sentences unfinished and even speaks without the benefit of connective syntax—"You ... you ... you ... brag ... brag ... bull ... bull" (131). Another indication of Mitch's insecurity and lack of confidence is his awkward reliance on the language of trite, conventional romance in wooing Blanche. He is so invested in the antiquated symbology of romance that it is easy for Blanche to trap, and then undercut, him. Among three of Mitch's many examples of stilted romancespeak are (1) "in all my experience I have never known any one like you" (87), a pickup line that serves as wonderful bait for Blanche's hook; (2) "you may teach school but you certainly are not an old maid" (56); and (3) perhaps his most disjunctively melodramatic line—"You need somebody. And I need somebody, too. Could it be—you and me, Blanche?" (96), cycling Mitch's banal sensitivity through the doubtful interrogative, the tentative.

Mitch's passing status in Blanche's life as well as his liabilities as a suitor are epitomized at the end of scene 5—Blanche "blows a kiss at [the newspaper boy] as he goes down the steps with a dazed look. She stands there dreamily after he has disappeared. Then Mitch appears around the corner with a bunch of roses" (84). A young, dashing rosenkavalier leaves Blanche's life as Mitch, the retreaded rosenkavalier, enters late, almost as an ominous second thought. Quite literally, Mitch is a runner-up who will run out of time in Blanche's world. His roses will be replaced by the Mexican woman's *flores*, the florilegia of grief.

Mitch's props of love are equally incomplete, cues to his amorous incompetence and failure. Blanche too easily snares him by asking for a cigarette (Murphy), thus giving Mitch an opportunity to recount his narrative about the deceased girl who loved him and then to produce the silver cigarette case with the poetic inscription "I shall love thee better after death." Mitch's past love affairs, like this one with Blanche, ended in defeat. He will never know recrudescence. He smokes Luckies, a choice that ironically and bluntly indicts him as "never getting lucky in love" and suggests that all sorts of sexual rituals/overtones go unfulfilled. The cigarette case he carries is equivalent to Blanche's trunk, the remnants of his former life—dead, unresurrectable. Mitch's narrative of self contains too many ghostly lacunae.

BRENDA MURPHY ON KAZAN'S PERCEPTION OF STEVE AND EUNICE

During the rehearsal period, Kazan developed the relationship of Steve and Eunice into a comic mirror for that of Stanley and Stella. Eunice's nagging at Steve for not telling her he was going bowling was a less attractive version of Stella's following Stanley around and going to watch him bowl. During the poker fight, Eunice expressed her objections to Steve more effectively if less delicately than Stella did hers to Stanley. When Eunice shouted down to Steve from her apartment, Steve muttered "Oh-oh!" and hurried upstairs (41). Kazan extended the fight between Steve and Eunice in scene 5 kinesically to show the kind of behavior Stanley expects from women. After their initial exchange about Steve's "going up" at the four deuces, Eunice appeared on the steps, a comic figure, "*rubbing her backside*" (53). When she returned with Steve from the Four Deuces after Stanley's initial accusation of Blanche, Eunice was sobbing, with Steve's arm around her, comforted by Steve's ludicrous explanation of why he saw other women: "You know I don't love those girls ... I love you. You know I love you. I only do that with other girls because I love you" (55).

Later in scene 5, as Steve and Eunice came out to meet Stanley, Kazan had Eunice race down the steps, bellowing "Come on, lover boy. Come on" (58) and shouting with laughter, Steve in hot pursuit. Stanley grabbed Eunice as she went by him, and she eluded him with delighted shrieks. When

Stella shrugged out of Stanley's grasp a moment later and walked coolly down the street, the contrast between the two women heightened Stanley's anger at the effect Blanche was having on his heretofore adoring and sensual wife. Kazan also encoded a reminder of the kind of relationship Stanley was missing in scene 8 after his explosion about the airs his women were putting on and his destruction of the dishes. As Stanley and Stella stood outside on the porch while Blanche tried to telephone Mitch, the audience heard "*laughter, at first quiet and intimate—and soon boisterous and downright dirty, between* EUNICE *and* STEVE *in the apartment above*" (77). It was at this point that Stanley made his plea to Stella that it was "gonna be all right again between you and me the way it was ... God, honey, it's gonna be sweet when we can make noise in the night the way that we used to and get the colored lights going with nobody's sister behind the curtains to hear us" (77–78).

Kazan also strengthened and dignified Eunice's character in some scenes, however, and emphasized her ties to Stella, partly to convey the extent to which Stella has become accustomed to the life of the Quarter and partly to encode a quality of natural human decency in the final scene. The play's opening scenic image of Stella sitting in the armchair eating candy from a paper bag, fanning herself, and reading a movie magazine, was mirrored in Eunice's sitting on the porch, eating peanuts and reading a confession magazine. The visual suggestion in this opening scene was that Stella was like any woman in the Quarter at this point. Eunice's casual intimacy with and loyalty to Stella was indicated in the first scene as she moved about the Kowalskis' apartment, putting away Stella's clothes and straightening up the beds, to defend her from Blanche's obvious disapproval. In the final scene Eunice was given additional dialogue to emphasize her and Stella's shared concern for Stella's baby, and it was she who held Stella in her arms and comforted her throughout the whole ordeal of Blanche's removal. Cutting Stella's line about the women of the Quarter being good-hearted and easy to get along with further tipped the balance of humanity in Eunice's favor. She is kind and loyal to Stella while Stella is disdainful and catty about her behind her back, at least when she is under Blanche's influence. Eunice may have appeared gross and ridiculous at times during the performance, but it was clear that she was the most decent person on the stage during the final scene.

In every case, Kazan's work with the actors served his basic purpose of objectifying the subjective, bringing the characters' individual perceptions of reality out in their behavior. It was at once the natural approach for a Method director to take toward actors and the appropriate direction for the subjective realism of *Streetcar*. As Williams said, the play was about the failure to communicate because of each character's failure to understand how the others saw the world. The tragic failure in the play was Chekhovian, the failure of four people to get beyond their subjective visions of the events both in the present and in the past so they can understand their significance to the others. Kazan's kinesic expression of that failure was the behavior of four people living out four separate visions of these events, their significance, and their consequences on the stage.

JACQUELINE O'CONNOR ON THE PATRIARCHY AND COMMITMENT OF FEMALES

The propensity for family members, often male, to arrange the commitment of female relatives, is noted by Yannick Ripa in her book *Women and Madness* (54–62). Although her book discusses nineteenth-century French women, many of her remarks present situations and attitudes appropriate to the time when Williams was writing. She notes that single women who were forced to work to support themselves were often more liable to be committed if they became unable to work. This is the situation Blanche faces at the opening of the play.

In scene seven, when Stanley tells Stella about what he has uncovered concerning Blanche's reputation in Laurel, he says that Blanche came to be regarded in her home town "as not just different but down right loco—nuts" (I, 361). Yet it is not until Blanche has been forced to resign her position as schoolteacher, and has come to reside in her sister's home, impoverished and without prospects for the future, that she is threatened with commitment. Ripa writes of the predicament of women who have no economic resources:

> spinsters who became mentally ill became embarrassing— financially if their mental illness meant that they were not able to work, but also morally because their presence was a stain on the family, disturbed it with their symptoms and raised the constant problem of "dangerousness." ... Nephews or brothers-in-law would therefore carry out the procedures necessary for commitment. (56)

In *Streetcar*, Blanche has come looking for asylum, and she has instead come to the place where she is most likely to end up in one. Recognition of the danger she faces as a penniless female suffering from nervous exhaustion is striking when Stanley and Stella first discuss her condition in scene two, but an exchange between Blanche and Stella in the opening scene foreshadows the conversation between the Kowalskis, especially in light of Ripa's remarks. When the sisters are talking about Blanche staying at the apartment rather than at a hotel, Blanche's claim that she must stay with them and "can't be alone" prompts Stella to remark, "You seem a little bit nervous or overwrought or something." Blanche rather incongruously counters with a question, "Will Stanley like me, or will I be just a visiting in-law, Stella?" (I, 257). Thus we see that Blanche's nervousness about whether she has found a refuge, and her insecurity about whether her brother-in-law will endure her presence, highlight her precarious position in the Kowalski home.

Other similarities link scenes two and seven, and lead to a better understanding of the way that Stella and Stanley conspire against Blanche. Significantly, these are the only two scenes in the play where Stanley and Stella have opportunities for private discussion, and in both, Blanche's mental state and her future dominate the dialogue.

In both scenes, Blanche is taking a bath, singing songs in which she provides an unwitting commentary on her condition while Stanley and Stella discuss it. In scene two, she sings: "From the land of the sky blue water,/ They brought a captive maid!" predicting her imminent captivity in the institution (I, 270). In addition, the "sky blue water" foreshadows her final long speech in the play, in which she speaks of dying at sea, her body "dropped overboard—at noon—in the blaze of summer— and into an ocean as blue as my first lover's eyes!" (I, 410). This connection is significant for a number of reasons, not only because madness is aligned with death, being a kind of death, a death of freedom, but also because Blanche's nervousness and instability are associated throughout the play with her marriage to the poet Allan Grey, the boy with those eyes.[6] So in her last speech of the play Blanche speaks of her death and her first lover, just before she is taken off to the asylum.

From the perspective of both stage reality and the dimensions of the Kowalski apartment, it is only while Blanche is in the bathroom that Stanley and Stella can speak privately, and only if she is singing and running water can they be certain to speak without her overhearing them. But Blanche singing of a "captive maid" while indulging in what she calls "hydrotherapy" at the same time that her sister and brother-in-law discuss her mental condition, comes down to more than just necessary staging; the scene forecasts what will happen later in the play.

In scene seven there are marked parallels to what the earlier scene introduced. Blanche is bathing again, and this time she is singing a song that includes the lyrics, "But it wouldn't be make-believe/ If you believed in me!" At that time, Stanley is insuring that Stella no longer believes in her, as he has already done with Mitch (I, 360). At one point the stage directions indicate that in the bathroom "the water goes on loud; little breathless cries and peals of laughter are heard as if a child were frolicking in the tub" (I, 362). As in the earlier scene, Stanley and Stella discuss Blanche while she is unaware. This conversation is more ominous than the first because Stanley informs Stella about her sister's promiscuity, the reason Blanche departed from Laurel, and his plans to send her on a bus back to the town she has been asked to leave. Although

Blanche never uses the ticket, it is significant that Stanley would fund her return, even though he knows she has been exiled from Laurel.

The final exchange between the two, before Blanche emerges from the bathroom, indicates that Stanley and Stella both realize that if Blanche cannot stay with them, and cannot return to her life in Laurel, something unmentionable awaits her in her future:

> *Stella* (slowly): What'll—she—do? What on earth will she—do!
> *Stanley*: Her future is mapped out for her.
> *Stella*: What do you mean? (I, 367)

At that point Stanley breaks off their conversation and calls for Blanche to get out of the bathroom. He does not answer his wife's question, and therefore leaves us wondering just what he thinks Blanche's future will contain. Although he is not specific, this exchange signals what is to come, for it is the Kowalskis who decide Blanche's fate, not Blanche herself. Her singing and giggling in the tub throughout this scene reveal how far she is from knowing what is being decided about her in the other room; however, the stage directions indicate that she registers fear, "almost a look of panic," when she does emerge from her bath, her hydrotherapy.

Besides the information these two scenes give us about her relatives will decide what is to become of her, both of these private talks between Stanley and Stella center on Blanche's economic condition, a condition inextricably tied to her family's power to decide her future. In scene two we discover that Blanche has lost the family home, Belle Reve, and so her situation is not only one of a woman suffering from nervous exhaustion, who has lost her income, it is of one who has also lost the place where she might have been able to shield herself from the censure of the community. The people of Laurel still might have regarded her as "downright loco—nuts," as Stanley puts it, but had she a place to live without danger of eviction, she might have remained in her hometown.

By coming to New Orleans and placing herself at the mercy of her relatives, admitting that she has lost Belle Reve, Blanche becomes economically vulnerable to Stanley's plans to extricate her from the apartment. This tie between economic dependence and the ability for others to commit her against her will becomes more strikingly apparent in scene seven, when Stanley emphasizes her joblessness—"She's not going back to teach school!" (I, 362); her homelessness—"They told her she better move on to some fresh territory" (I, 363); and his decision to expel her from the premises—"She's not staying here after Tuesday" (I, 367).

Notes
6. Yannick Ripa suggests that in the popular imagination madness was often seen as a "punishment better than death, which would be too much. It was a half-death, the death of the mind" (2).

NICHOLAS PAGAN ON
THE SIGNIFICANCE OF NAMES

"Stella for Star" is the first of a number of astronomical/astrological; references in a play that was once entitled *Blanche's Chair in the Moon*, a play where a newsboy sells papers for "The Evening Star" (Blanche jokes "I didn't know stars took up collections" [82]), and where Blanche looks in the sky for "the Pleiades, the Seven Sisters" (86). With Stanley, Blanche will discuss astrological signs, indicating that her birthday is on the fifteenth of September and that she is therefore "a Virgo." "What's Virgo?" asks Stanley. Blanche explains "Virgo is the Virgin" (77). Here Blanche, inadvertently perhaps, is also making sense of her name. In a sense, she is speaking out of her name, for to be a virgin is to be untouched, pure, clean, as in *virgin snow*. This is not to say that Blanche is a virgin, but through her name, she is linked to whiteness and to virginity. During the Poker Night scene, Blanche glosses her own name when meeting Mitch for the first time:

Mitch. Deal me out, I'm talking to Miss—
Blanche. DuBois.
Mitch. Miss DuBois?
Blanche. It's a French name. It means woods and Blanche
means white, so the two together mean white woods.
Like an orchard in spring! You can remember it by
that.

(54–55)

Of course, Blanche's commentary here is inaccurate because "white woods" in French would be *bois blanc*. If the adjective and noun are to be taken together as Blanche suggests, they should agree with each other in terms of gender; in other words, the adjective *blanche* would have to be *blanc* to agree with the noun *bois*, which is masculine.[65] Thus, the name Blanche DuBois presents us with a confusion of gender.

In English the verb "to blanch" can mean "1. to take the color out of and make white: BLEACH.... 2. to make ashen or pale.... 3. to give a favorable appearance to: WHITEWASH, GLOSS—often used with over" (*Webster's*). Of course, I am making use here of homophones, that is words that sound alike even though their meanings may be different. When we hear the name, Blanche, then we may hear the verb "blanch," and we can think of Blanche blanching—trying to make her world white, pure, innocent, virginal; trying to gloss, to gloss over.[66]

Blanche is blanching, for both in her name and in her language, she is constantly glossing, in the sense of giving explanations or interpretations (for example, "Stella, Stella for Star" or "white woods" for Blanche DuBois). To gloss can also mean "to veil or hide [something that would otherwise be objected to or prove a source of difficulty] by some plausible pretext, subterfuge, pretense or excuse" (*Webster's*). Despite her claim, "I've nothing to hide" (40), Blanche always seems to be hiding something. In fact, she is hiding the confusion of gender and sexual orientation in her name. Although Blanche is obviously female, she can also be seen as male.

George Michelle Sarotte points out that although novels containing homosexuals were acceptable when *A Streetcar*

Named Desire first appeared in 1947 it was not acceptable to have homosexual characters appear on or even off-stage.[67] It was more acceptable for homosexual characters to appear in fiction. Williams then, focuses more directly on the homosexual in his short stories—for example, "The Mysteries of the Joy Rio" (1941), "The Angel in the Alcove" (1943), "The Resemblance between a Violin Case and a Coffin" (written in 1949), "Hard Candy" (begun in 1949, finished in 1953), and "One Arm" (begun in 1942, finished in 1945). Stanley Hyman, however, has suggested that Williams employs "the Albertine Strategy," that is to say, disguises homosexual males as females as Proust had done in changing the name Albert to Albertine in *A la recherche du temps perdu*."[68]

Notice that Stanley Kowalski offers us the possibility of reading Blanche as gay male when he says, "What *queen* do you think you are?" (emphasis added; 127) Even the first audiences of *A Streetcar Named Desire* may have been aware of the homosexual connotations of the term "queen." "Homosexual" is one meaning of "queen" given by the *New Dictionary of American Slang*: "A male homosexual, especially one who ostentatiously takes a female role." According to this dictionary, the homosexual sense of "queen" appeared as early as the late nineteenth century. There is evidence that in 1949, Tennessee Williams himself was using the term "queen" in the homosexual sense. In a letter to Maria St. Just dated 9 October 1949, Williams writes: "Well, the town is blooming with British queens, mostly connected in some way with the ballet."[69]

Similarly, Mitch's observation, "I was fool enough to believe you was *straight*" (emphasis added; 117) can make us think of Blanche as not straight, as homosexual. The *Dictionary of American Slang* defines the adjective "straight" as "1. Undiluted, neat; said of liquor. 2. Honest; normal. Depending on the context, denotes that the person referred to is not dishonest, not a drug addict, not a homosexual, and so forth." The Dictionary further specifies that the uses "sexually normal and/or not a drug-addict" have been employed since 1945. Thus, we may infer that like "queen" the sexual connotations of "straight" may have been familiar to the first audiences of *A Streetcar Named Desire*. Although we may feel that Mitch means that he thought that Blanche was honest, we can still hear "straight" as heterosexual. In her numerous sexual experiences with boys, Blanche may be regarded as both heterosexual woman often described by critics as "nymphomaniac" and as gay male. The name Blanche DuBois, then, opens up confusions of gender and sexuality that it is difficult to deny.

In English "blanch" can also mean "to bleach by excluding light" (*Webster's*). Rarely leaving the apartment in the daytime, Blanche is a creature of the night. "Her delicate beauty must avoid a strong light" (15). She claims that she cannot endure the sight of "a naked light bulb" (55). Living in darkness, she becomes increasingly pale (blanch), as white perhaps as the clothes that she wore when she first arrived: white suit, gloves, and hat (15), but one has the feeling that the whiteness of her clothes and her name hide something, something dark. She is attracted to innocence, just as a moth is attracted to the light. We know, however, that Blanche is no virgin. She has freely given herself, her whiteness (including her virginity) to the boys; but for the most part, she conceals this fact, hides it beneath her white apparel and beneath her name.

Her name may also be appropriate for her marriage may never have been consummated and would therefore be *une marriage blanche*. This is clearer in the movie version of the play. Gene Phillips points out that for Kazan's movie version, Williams had to rewrite Blanche's speech about Allan Grey in order to tone down the homosexuality—in other words, to avoid the reference to Blanche finding her young husband in bed with another man.[70] Instead, in the movie, then, Blanche describes how on their wedding night she pretended to sleep but heard Allan crying. With the implication that Allan is impotent in the marital bed, the possibility of his being gay is not erased and the possibility of *une marriage blanche* is more striking than in the play.

Of course, there is apart of Blanche that wants to appear "virginal," "white," *blanche*, a "lily."[71] But the other side of Blanche wants to speak, refuses to hold back, refuses to remain

110

silent, insists that she is no virgin. In French, *blanche* means white, but it is also the musical term in French for a half note. Furthermore, isn't *blanche* a combination of *bl* and the French *anche* which means "reed," a rustic musical pipe. Moreover, Blanche tells Mitch that in French bois "means woods and Blanche means white, so the two together mean white woods. Like an orchard in spring!" (SND, 55). This wood in Blanche's name pulls together all the references, not just to woods but orchards and trees and branches and leaves and twigs that we have seen scattered throughout Williams's texts and pre-texts.

Notice also that Blanche imagines the area outside the Kowalski apartment to be "the ghoul-haunted woodland of Weir!" (SND, 20). Given her name, how appropriate that Blanche DuBois, Blanche of the Wood, should imagine a wood even in the heart of New Orleans. The reference, of course, in to Edgar Allen Poe's "Ulalume—A Ballad," another possible pre-text in which a poet grieves the death of a loved one. Describing this poem in *The Encyclopedia Britannica*, Theodore Watts-Danton suggests that "the poet's object ... was to express dull and hopeless gloom in the same way that the mere musician would have expressed it—that is to say, by monotonous reiterations, by hollow and dreadful reverberations of gloomy sounds.... 'Ulalume' properly intoned would produce something like the same effect upon a listener knowing no word of English that it produces upon us."[72] Both musically and thematically, the leaves which are "crisped and sere," may be like those at the end of *The Glass Menagerie*, and the cypress trees like those in Battle of Angels. Poe's poem fits neatly into the intertextual network established here. Curiously, in French, *bois* can also refer to the woodwind instruments or section of the orchestra. Thus through the *blanche* (half note), *anche* (reed) and *bois* (wood + woodwind instrument), Blanche DuBois seems inextricably tied both to woods (trees), music, and Orpheus.

In "The Garrulous Grotesques of Tennessee Williams," Ruby Cohn points out that "anglicized Blanche's name is Duboys, and under her chaste surface, Blanche lusts for boys."[73] Blanche frequently refers to her husband as a boy. At

111

the end of scene 1, Blanche tells Stanley, "The boy—the boy died" (SND, 31). In the next scene she protects Allan's letter, "Poems a dead boy wrote," from the touch of Stanley's hands (42). Even Stella forces us to see that Allan was only a boy: "she [Blanche] married a boy who wrote poetry" (102). After the death of "the Grey Boy" (96), Blanche used to entertain the young soldiers returning to barracks after a night on the town (120). Later, after "many intimacies with strangers," she lost her job at the school because of an involvement with a seventeen-year-old boy (118). She is clearly attracted to the newsboy in scene 5 and to Stanley who refers to himself as a boy in scene 10. ("Not once did you pull any wool over this *boy's* eyes!" [emphasis added; 127]). And then in the last scene of the play, she muses wistfully about a young doctor who she dreams will be by her bedside the night she dies (136). It seems very appropriate then to read Blanche DuBois as Blanche DuBoys—Blanche of or from the boys.[74]

This reading of Blanche DuBoys as Blanche DuBoys also provides further ground for seeing in Blanche an allusion to Orpheus. In Virgil's *Georgic* IV, Orpheus's rejection of or indifference toward the women who are attracted to him can be seen, as suggested by Emmett Robbins, as "simply the result of the singer's undying attachment to the woman he has lost."[75] W.K.C. Guthrie points out, however, that following the loss of Eurydice, and his subsequent shunning of the company of women, "he [Orpheus] did not avoid the report which so often attaches to those who lead celibate lives, of having another outlet for his passions."[76] For some commentators, Orpheus therefore became "the originator of homosexual love."[77] Ovid leaves us in little doubt concerning Orpheus's sexual relations with boys, for we are told that while "Orpheus held himself / Aloof from love of women ... / It was his lead that taught the folk of Thrace / The love for tender boys" (MET, 227).[78] Therefore, through her actions as a lover of boys, and through her name, Blanche DuBoys, Blanche DuBoys, Blanche may again be seen as alluding to Orpheus.

If we look back for a moment to the trees that gather around Orpheus, we may observe that two of the last to join the group are a pine tree, formerly the young Attis, and a cypress, formerly the young Cyparissus, both boys loved by gods. W.S. Anderson concludes that in Ovid's account, Orpheus' song "features pretty young boys, not Eurydice."[79] Orpheus, who teaches "the love for tender boys" is, like Blanche, the seducer of boys. Now it seems that Blanche is closer both through her name and actions to Orpheus, than Val is to Orpheus. In *Battle of Angels* and *Orpheus Descending*, Val shows no signs of attraction to young boys. In fact, the emphasis in the play is on how others are attracted to him. Notice that he is also frequently described as boy. In *Battle of Angels*, Myra reads Val's letter of recommendation from an old employer in which the employer says, "This here boy's peculiar" (BA, 147). Lady tells Val early in *Orpheus Descending*, "Boys like you don't work" (OD, 48). Near the end of that play, Talbott warns Val: "Boy, don't let the sun rise on you in this county" (OD 121). Were Val to be transplanted from *Orpheus Descending* to *A Streetcar Named Desire*, there is no doubt that Blanche would desire him. She may be like Virgil's Orpheus, constantly mourning the loss of her young love (in her case a boy), but like Ovid's Orpheus, she is also the lover of boys and in this role may be regarded as a stand-in for Tennessee Williams.

Notes

65. It is, perhaps, no coincidence that the same lack of agreement in terms of gender occurs in the name of the former DuBois family estate Belle Reve. The noun *reve* meaning "dream" should be preceded by the masculine form of the adjective, *beau*.

66. Williams makes repeated use of the verb *blanch*. See, for example, the beginning of Nono's poem in *The Night of the Iguana*:

How Calmly does the orange branch
Observe the sky begin to blanch
Without a cry, without a prayer,
With no betrayal of despair
(NI, 123)

67. *Like A Brother*, pp. 108–109.

68. Stanley Edgar Hyman, "Some Notes on the Albertine Strategy," *Hudson Review* 6 (Autumn 1953): 417–22.

69. Maria St. Just, *Five O'Clock Angel: Letters of Tennessee Williams to Maria St. Just 1948–1982* (New York: Alfred Knopf, 1990), p. 26.

70. Gene D. Phillips, *The Films of Tennessee Williams* (Philadelphia: Art Alliance Press, 1980), pp. 81–82.

71. In scene 7, Stanley laughs at the idea of Blanche as a lily. "But Sister Blanche is no lily! Ha-ha! Some lily she is!" (99). One definition of lily is "one that resembles the lily in whiteness, fairness, purity, or fragility" [a virgin, a most unspotted—{Shak.}]" (*Webster's*).

72. Quoted in Edgar Allan Poe, *The Poems of Edgar Allan Poe*, ed. Killis Cambell (New York: Russel and Russel, 1962), p. 272.

73. Ruby Cohn, "The Garrulous Grotesques of Tennessee Williams," in *Tennessee Williams: A Collection of Critical Essays*, ed. Stephen S. Stanton (Englewood Cliffs, N.J.: Prentice-Hall, 1977), p. 46. Notice, also, that the name DuBois is occasionally pronounced Du Boy as in the name, W.E.B. Du Bois.

74. Blanche DuBois is not the only one of Williams's characters who appears in a play where language suggests that she may be read as being a boy. Such a reading is even more obvious for Maggie in *Cat on a Hot Tin Roof*. Maggie is described as having a voice that "sometimes ... drops as low as a boy's and you have a sudden image of her playing boy's games as a child" (CT, 18). Furthermore, like Blanche Maggie calls her husband a boy: "I'll tell you what they're up to, boy of mine!" (CT, 17). Brick's body is described as "still slim and firm as a boy" (CT, 17), and following his relationship with Skipper there are question marks surrounding his sexuality.

75. Emmet Robbins, "Famous Orpheus," in *Orpheus: The Metamorphosis of a Myth*, ed. John Warden (Toronto and Buffalo: University of Toronto Press, 1982), p. 14.

76. W.K.C. Gurthrie, *Orpheus and the Greek Religion: A Study of the Orphic Movement* (New York: Norton, 1966), pp. 31–32.

77. Ibid., p. 32.

78. The editor, here, E.J. Kenny, points out that the "tradition" of Orpheus's "love for tender boys" was "attested by the Alexandrian poet Phanocles." Kenny also says that "Sandys found the lines too shocking to translate" (MET, p. 432 n. 84).

79. "The Orpheus of Ovid and Virgil: *flebile nesquio quid*," in *Orpheus: The Metamorphoses of a Myth*, ed. John Warden (Toronto: The University of Toronto Press, 1982), p. 45.

Nicholas Pagan on the Significance of Music in Characterization

Many of the possible Orphic parallels and connections with the blues that I have just explored in some of the early plays come together in *A Streetcar Named Desire*. Instead of the "blue guitar" of earlier plays, music is provided, in particular, by a "blue piano." Never one to mince words, Elia Kazan says that "the blue piano catches the soul of Blanche," and he argues that "the blues is an expression of the loneliness and rejection, the exclusion and isolation of the Negro and their opposite longing for love and connection. Blanche too is 'looking for a home,' abandoned, friendless. 'I don't know where I'm going, but I'm going.'"[56] We should not, however, see the blues as exclusively belonging to Blanche, any more than the blues is exclusively the Sister's in *The Purification*. In that play, the blues also reflected the feelings of the brother. In *A Streetcar Named Desire*, the blues is linked at different times to many of the characters. In scene 3, for example, after Stanley's outburst during the poker game, the black musicians around the corner play a song called "Paper Doll." They play it "slow and blue." Stanley has lost Stella, his "baby doll." As he tries to call upstairs, "the 'blue piano' plays for a brief interval." Eventually, slowly, and with the sound of "low clarinet moans" in the background, Stella comes down the staircase, and Stanley "falls to his knees on the steps and presses his face to her belly, curving a little with maternity" (SND, 60). The scene may recall to some, the Son's comment about the musician in *The Purification*:

> His song, which is truth
> is not to be captured ever.
> It is an image, a dream,
> It is the link to the mother ...
> (27W, 40)

The blues music here in *A Streetcar Named Desire* may be depicting the inevitability of separation of mother and baby—

115

with Stanley as the crying baby losing his mother, Stella, whose belly is "curving a little with maternity." At other moments in the play, the blues may be played for Stella. The "blue piano" music in scene 7 can be associated with Stella's feelings about losing the Blanche she once knew. At the end of the play, holding her baby wrapped in a pale blue blanket, Stella cries out her sister's name three times, "Blanche! Blanche! Blanche!" (SND, 142). This reminds me of the moment in Virgil's text when the name, Eurydice, is heard three times as Orpheus's dismembered head floats down the Hebrus to the sea:

> Its death-cold tongue cried forth "Eurydice!"
> The parting breath sighed "Poor Eurydice!"
> "Eurydice!" the sounding shores replied.
> (GEV 119–20)[57]

Stella goes out on to the porch and "sobs with inhuman abandon." "There is something luxurious," we are told, "in her complete surrender to crying now that her sister is gone" (SND, 142). Although the Son in *The Purification* has to live with the death of his sister, Stella too loses a sister—this time not to death, but to the madhouse.[58] In spite of these possibilities, however, Kazan is right to suggest that the blues is essentially Blanche's music. The "blue piano" is playing throughout scene 1, but the music grows louder when Blanche describes the loss of Belle Reve. The music may represent Blanche's loneliness and exclusion from the conjugal scene in scenes 2, 4, and 5 because in scene 2, Stanley announces Stella's pregnancy; in scene 4 Stanley and Stella embrace as Stanley grins through the curtains at Blanche; and in scene 5 Steve and Eunice chase each other, and Stella and Stanley go off arm in arm. Her exclusion from the family scene is also marked in scene 9 where Mitch tells her that she "is not even clean enough to bring in the house with [his] mother" (SND, 121). The "blue piano" may also point to her loneliness in scene 8 when Mitch fails to show up for Blanche's birthday supper, and in scene 10 when Shep Huntleigh fails to materialize.

The "blue piano" may also be seen as providing background music to remind us of the great loss that Blanche, like Orpheus, has had to endure: the loss of a young love. The "blue piano" is heard at the crucial moment in the newsboy scene when the boy is looking for a way out. "Young man! Young man, young man!," says Blanche, "Has anyone ever told you that you look like a young Prince out of the Arabian Nights?" (SND, 84). The repetitions of the word "young" may remind us of her young love Allan Grey, "The Grey Boy" (SND, 96).

As *A Streetcar Named Desire* draws to a close, then, when we hear "the swelling music of the 'blue piano' and the muted trumpet" (SND, 142), we should think of the blues as primarily Blanche's music. Although the action of the play takes place in "Elysian Fields," Blanche has not found paradise, the "heavenly grass" of which Val sang. Like Val, like Orpheus, the archetypal poet of the West, Blanche has no home; and like the characters in Samuel Beckett's *Waiting for Godot* or Williams's own late play, *The Two-Character Play*, she has no place to which she can escape: she has quite simply nowhere to go.

Williams announces in his introduction to *A Streetcar Named Desire*, "On a Streetcar Named Success," that "the monosyllable of the clock is Loss, Loss, Loss, unless you devote your heart to its opposition," and loss is indeed a central concern of both Orpheus and Blanche. Orpheus loses his Eurydice (in fact, he loses her twice—at the beginning of the story she is already lost and then with the fateful look back he loses her again). Blanche loses her Allan Grey. These losses cause Orpheus and Blanche incalculable sadness, and to express this sadness words alone are inadequate, and hence the need for music.

In *Conversation with the Blues*, Paul Oliver transcribes several interviews that he has had with blues musicians, and tries to establish a definition of the blues. Lil Son Jackson comments

> Well I think the blues is more or less a feeling that you get from something that you think is wrong, or something that somebody did wrong to you.... That's the way I see the blues. It cause a sad feeling, more or less a

sad feeling about it, and when you have that sad feeling well, quite naturally you reproduce it.[59]

Of course, Blanche thinks that she has done something wrong. She feels guilty about telling Allan that he disgusted her—for this provoked his suicide, and Blanche is haunted by this, not only through the blues but also through the polka music and the sound of the gunshot. Surely, Orpheus feels that he has been wronged by those who have taken away his Eurydice, and perhaps he feels too that he must share in the responsibility for the loss that followed his fateful look back.

Also in *Conversation with the Blues*, Edwin Buster Pickens maintains that

> The only way anyone can ever play blues—he's got to have them.... No man in good spirit, no man in good heart can sing the blues, neither play them.... But nach'al blues come directly from a person's heart.... You have a tough way in life—that makes you blue. That's when you start to sing the blues, when you've got the blues.[60]

In his "Historical and Critical Text" that accompanies W.C. Handy's *A Treasury of the Blues*, Abbe Niles suggests that as far as the blues is concerned,

> the essential element is the singer's own personality. Whatever is said is in some way brought back to him; he deals in his own troubles, desires, resentments, his opinions of life and people. There seems even to be room left for his pleasures. Happy blues are rare, but some have an invincible optimism ... Melancholy, however, is most frequently the theme; there is no doubt that the name "blues" was bestowed on the tunes because of the mood of the verses.[61]

In *A Streetcar Named Desire*; Blanche is the character melancholy enough to sing the blues. She is the character who suffers most the pangs of lost love. She is the character, like

Orpheus, who has no home. She is the character who has the most experience of solitude. Perhaps the song that she sings in the bathtub could be sung to a blues accompaniment. Like many blues ballads, "It's Only a Paper Moon" combines the lament for lost love with the feeling that without that love the world is phony:

> Without your love,
> It's a honkey-tonk parade!
> Without your love,
> It's a melody played
> In a penny arcade
> . . . .
> It's only a paper moon,
> just as phony as it can be—
> But it wouldn't be make-believe
> If you believed in me!
> . . . .
> It's a Barnum and Bailey World,
> Just as phony as it
> can be—
>   (SND, 100–101)

As Stanley and Stella hear her singing and the sound of running water, they can also hear "little breathless cries and peals of laughter ... as if a child were frolicking in the tub" (SND, 101). They might wonder whether Blanche's gaiety is feigned, "phony," like the world depicted in the song, or is this one of those rare happy blues? Undoubtedly, Blanche has "got the blues." With her song, "It's Only a Paper Moon," perhaps we can hear some of that "invincible optimism" that Abbe Niles talked about. Perhaps Blanche attempts to cover up her profound and ineluctable sadness, but according to LeRoi Jones, "the blues, as it came into its own strict form, was the most plaintive and melancholy music imaginable."[62] Not only does the blues clearly retain this plaintive and melancholy aspect today, but these were also the characteristics of Orphic music. Orpheus may have been the first musician, but the blues may be as old as his music. Blues artist Boogie Woogie Red explains

> I'll tell you about the blues—the blues is something that you play when you're in a low mood or something.... And the average person takes the blues as just a plaything, but the blues is really serious. The blues is something that you have to play coming from your heart. And blues have been goin' on for centuries and centuries, and the blues was written years and centuries ago—they was always here.[63]

I am suggesting, then, that there is a place for the playwright in the intertextual network that brings together the blues and the Orphic. The adjectives that spring to mind here are plaintive, melancholy, and relentless. The intertextual resonances that I have established here may provide us with more accurate pointers to the author's biographical self than traditional source studies would. A part of the intertextual network, however, still needs to be examined, and that is the part to which we now turn our attention: the suggestiveness of the proper name.

Notes

56. Elia Kazan, "Notebook for *A Streetcar Named Desire*," in *Directors on Directing: A Source Book for Modern Theater*, eds. Toby Cole and Helen Krick Chinoy (Indianapolis and New York: Bobbs-Merril, 1976), p. 371.

57. Notice also that in *The Divine Comedy*, Dante marks the moment of Virgil's departure with the triple repetition of his name: "But Virgil had deprived us of himself, / Virgil, the gentlest father, Virgil he / to whom I gave myself for my salvation' (*The Divine Comedy of Dante Alighieri: Purgatorio*, trans. Allen Mandelbaum [New York: Bantam, 1984], bk. Xxx, pp. 49–51).

58. The inevitability of such losses is articulated by Joe in *The Long Goodbye*. He expresses his gloomy philosophy to his friend, Silva: "You're saying good-bye all the time, every minute you live." Because that's what life is, just a long, long good-bye—to one thing after another! Till you get to the last one, Silva, and that's—goodbye to yourself." (27W, 178).

59. Paul Oliver, *Conversation with the Blues* (New York: Horizon Press, 1986), p. 170.

60. Ibid.

61. W.C. Handy, ed. *A Treasury of the Blues: Complete Words and Music of 67 Great songs from Memphis to the Present Day with an Historical and Critcal Text by Abbe Niles* (new York: Charles Boni, 1949), p. 11.

62. *Blues People*, p. 78.

63. Quoted in Oliver, *Conversation with the Blues*, p. 25.

LEONARD QUIRINO ON THE METAPHOR OF GAMES AND CARDS

"Catch!" (I, 244) says Stanley Kowalski throwing a bloodstained package of meat to his wife, Stella, at the opening of the first scene of *A Streetcar Named Desire*. Laughing breathlessly, she manages to catch it. "This game is seven-card stud," reads the last line of the play. In between, much of the verbal and theatrical imagery that constitutes the drama is drawn from games, chance and luck. Williams had called the short play from which *Streetcar* evolved *The Poker Night*, and in the final version two of the most crucial scenes are presented within the framework of poker games played onstage. Indeed, the tactics and ceremonial of games in general, and poker in particular, may be seen as constituting the informing structural principle of the play as a whole. Pitting Stanley Kowalski, the powerful master of Elysian Fields against Blanche DuBois, the ineffectual ex-mistress of Belle Reve, Williams makes the former the inevitable winner of the game whose stakes are survival in the kind of world the play posits. For the first four of the eleven scenes of *Streetcar*, Blanche, by reason of her affectation of gentility and respectability, manages to bluff a good hand in her game with Stanley; thus, in the third scene Stanley is continually losing, principally to Mitch the potential ally of Blanche, in the poker game played onstage. However, generally suspicious of Blanche's behavior and her past, and made aware at the end of the fourth scene that she considers him an ape and a brute, Stanley pursues an investigation of the real identity of *her* cards. As, little by little, he finds proof of what he considers her own apishness and brutality, he continually discredits her gambits until, in the penultimate scene, he caps his winnings by raping her. In the last scene of the play, Stanley is not only winning every card game being played onstage, but he has also won the game he played with Blanche. Depending as it does on the skillful manipulation of the hands that chance deals out, the card game is used by Williams throughout *Streetcar* as a symbol of fate and of the skillful player's ability to make its decrees perform in his own favor at the expense of his opponent's misfortune, incompetence, and horror of the game itself.

Equally as important as the symbol of the card game in *Streetcar* is the imagery connected with the mythic archetype of the voyage which Williams portrays both as quest for an imagined ideal and as flight from disillusioning actuality. "They told me," says Blanche in her first speech, "to take a streetcar named Desire, and then to transfer to one called Cemeteries and ride six blocks and get off at—Elysian Fields." Putting together the allegorical names of these streetcars and their destination at Elysian Fields with Williams' portrayal of Blanche as resembling a moth, traditionally a symbol of the soul, we find in her journey a not too deeply submerged metaphor for the soul's disastrous voyage through life. Caged in a body that it attempts to transcend but cannot escape, the moth-soul yearns for the star (Stella) and for rest in the isles of the happy dead; it finds, instead, the flaming "red hot" milieu of the primal blacksmith ("Stanley" or "stone-lea" suggests the Stone Age man and "Kowalski" is Polish for "smith") and a world even more blatantly dedicated to "epic fornications" than its native Belle Reve, a world that shows every sign of prevailing. We are not surprised to learn that the agent of Blanche's journey to Elysian Fields, her school superintendent, is a Mr. Graves, and we can understand the implications of Blanche's statement late in the play, "The opposite [of death] is desire," to be more than merely sexual. Shuttling between yearning and frustration defines the basic rhythm of life itself for Blanche. Opening with her arrival in the land of life in death, the play chronicles the human soul's past and present excursions in the only vehicle that fate provides her, the rattle-trap streetcar of the body; the play closes with the soul's departure for incarceration in another asylum, another kind of living death.

JOHN M. RODERICK ON STANLEY AS A PSYCHOLOGICAL HERO

On a purely psychological level rather than a social one, however, Stanley emerges as hero. The sexually healthy marriage he shares with Stella stands as the sacred arena defiled by the profane intruder Blanche with her sexual perversity. If Stanley is taken at his word when he confides in Stella, the normalcy of their relationship is convincing: "Stell, it's gonna be all right after she goes and after you've had the baby.... God, honey, it's gonna be sweet when we can make noise in the night the way that we used to and get the colored lights going with nobody's sister behind the curtain to hear us. (Their upstairs neighbors are heard in bellowing laughter at something. Stanley chuckles.) Steve an' Eunice ..." (p. 373). And if we believe that any good subplot is a crucial reflection of the grain of the main plot, then Stanley's allusion to Steve and Eunice also fortifies the position that the Kowalskis share a successful marriage. The relationship of the couple upstairs parallels the marriage of Stanley and Stella in every way—from the violent outbursts to the sensual compensations. Even after the Kowalskis' violent argument, Mitch assures Blanche, "There's nothing to be scared of. They're crazy about each other" (p. 308). Steve and Eunice are likewise able to brook such battles.

In direct contrast to Stanley, on the other hand, Blanche represents the epitome of a psychological malaise. Her sexual perversions with schoolboys are in direct contrast to the normalcy of Stanley's aggressive sexuality in marriage. In the role of psychological profaner, Blanche as much as Stanley is to blame for the rape: "We've had this date with each other from the beginning!" (p. 402), he ominously tells Blanche just before he rapes her. And both he and Blanche recognize the truth in his statement. Earlier Blanche confided to Mitch, "The first time I laid eyes on him I thought to myself, that man is my executioner! That man will destroy me, unless—" (p. 351). Similarly, it is against Blanche as profane intruder into his domain as "a richly feathered male bird among hens," that Stanley violently reacts as his role of supremacy is threatened in his own house. When Stella tells him to help clear the table, "He hurls a plate to the floor," and says, "That's how I'll clear the table! (He seizes her arm) Don't ever talk that way to me! 'Pig—Polack—disgusting—vulgar—greasy!'— them kind of words have been on your tongue and your sister's too much around here! What do you two think you are? A pair of queens? ... (He hurls a cup and saucer to the floor) My place is cleared! You want me to clear your places?" (p. 371). Psychologically speaking, then, Blanche represents the profanation of Stanley's sacred, if crude, marriage. But we must cope with both the social and the psychological levels simultaneously. Thus the ambiguous duality in our appraisal of Stanley and Blanche is encouraged by Williams, an ambiguity which is not central to the; genre of traditional tragedy alone.

NANCY TISCHLER ON STANLEY AND BLANCHE AS ANTI-THETICAL IDEALS

The generalization that would grow naturally out of this contrasted analysis of two extremely different Williams plays is clearly that Williams should restrict himself to slightly altered reminiscences. However, another powerfully written play suggests more interestingly the boundaries of Tennessee Williams' talents. *A Streetcar Named Desire* uses many of these same materials with astonishing and effective variations. The story is again one of family tensions, the demands of the past impinging on the present, culture facing barbarism, sickness threatening health, man fighting woman. Yet, while it is much more violent than *Glass Menagerie*, *Streetcar* is much more real and much more tragic than *Battle of Angels*.

The wanderer entering alien territory is again sensitive and artistic and morally suspect. But it is a woman who takes the role of guardian of human values this time. Her age, her accent, her memories, and her demands on those who love her remind the reader of Amanda. But Blanche contains within her character much that reminds one of Tom as well. She too finds the past stifles her, she too searches for a new life that has beauty and adventure. And she is more forthright in the admission that one is never free of the past. It is always part of one's luggage. Blanche contains more of Williams' self than does Amanda. While the playwright saw the earlier character with sympathy and irony combined, he more fully identifies with the later character. Critics have frequently noted Williams' remarkable ability to create fully rounded female characters. The reason is largely that it is in the woman or the effeminate man that Williams most often reveals himself. Blanche, like Williams, lives briefly in New Orleans, her accent and her manners contrast grotesquely with those about her, her love of romance seems ludicrous to the world she can never quite bring herself to enter. In the feminine personality, Williams has found his satisfying parallel to the Romantic poet; in our culture, love of beauty is seen as a weakness in a man, excessive sensitivity as a fault.

The antithesis is Stanley Kowalski—all that society worships in the male. He is virile, loud, smart, aggressive, ambitious, and independent. He is in fact the sum total of those characteristics Williams resented in his father, and his portrait explains the omission of the father from *Menagerie*. Stanley's view of Blanche parallels society's view of the artist. He resents the implicit judgment on his own habits of mind and life. He resents the intrusion into his world of this alien voice. And he feels threatened by the strength behind the veneer of weakness. Therefore he attacks her with his natural weapons, stripping her of her illusive surface; he turns the naked bulb on her to reveal her physical weaknesses. He isolates her from her lover and her sister, and then rapes her and sends her off to the madhouse. His role is essentially the same as that of the men in *Battle of Angels*. This time, though, the brutality is more effective because of the difference in sex. Rather than attributing the men's hatred of the Romantic to some mystique of sex envy that forces the actor playing the sensitive poet to flex his muscles and lounge suggestively around the stage while stroking his guitar, Williams allows the more complex antipathy between the lover of the ideal and the lover of the real to be his motive for destruction.

Rape is a more effective image for what society does to the artist than lynching. In *Orpheus Descending*, the characters toy with the idea of castration, and in *Sweet Bird of Youth*, they carry out their threat. Williams here points out that this is, what life and time do to all of us, but to the most sensitive first. Rape is an effective term for what the Romantic believes the world does to him and his art. It robs the artist of his dreams and then uses him for its own diversion. In Holden Caulfield's terms, it prostitutes the artist.

Madness is also a good image for Williams' Romantic ideal, for the world must look on the poet's retreat from its vision of reality as madness. It is not surprising that Williams so often cites Don Quixote as one of his literary heroes. Their theories of madness are remarkably similar.

In *Streetcar*, Williams is able to present in Blanche, even more effectively than earlier in Tom, certain features of his self-portrait. The mask releases him from his pugilistic stance and allows him to admit partial acceptance of his mother's values. Now he can show sympathetically the doomed, beauty of the past contrasted with the gross vitality of the present, and the baroque rhetoric of the South compared with the grunts of the animalistic realist. He can confess his love of fragility without sounding sentimental. And he can insist (perhaps protesting overmuch) that his moral "corruption" has a reason and a history, and he can show that it carries with it consequent tortures. He can also admit an ambiguity in his relation to Stanley and his virile world of poker, drink, raw meat, and raw sex. Blanche's flirtation is as real as her disgust. She courts her own disaster; the death-wish, a need for punishment, for self-destruction may be a partial explanation. But the later love–hate between Brick and Big Daddy suggests still another: that the artist secretly admires and even loves the caveman who threatens his existence.

The most curious point of all seems to be a confession that Blanche's world and his are doomed. One can escape only into death, madness, or chaos. In *Camino Real*, his heroes are all diminished but still undefeated Romantics—Byron, Don Quixote, Camille—who have found that the Royal Road turns into the Real Road at the border. Like the Princess in *Sweet Bird of Youth*, they are now in Ogre Country, where their defeat, though inevitable, can yet be heroic. Williams clearly damns the real world, but he finds no escape from it that lasts for long.

Blanche's story is less believable than Tom's, but her character is much more fully realized. Williams' real talent lies not in construction, but in understanding, in characterization rather than in plotting. *Streetcar* contains many of the ambiguities discovered in *Battle of Angels*, but a character study needs less consistency and clarity than does a sermon. Blanche is no idealized heroine. Williams allows the real person to carry the burden of the meaning. Her quest is for love and beauty, as was Val's, her weariness with corruption echoes his, but Williams does not outfit her in outlandish mythic garb, idealize her journey, or insist on her apotheosis. As a self-portrait she is more natural, more honest, and more tragic than any Williams character before or since. She embodies his sense of isolation, his concern for cruelty, his dread of death, and his disgust with his own flesh. She may be dypsomaniac and nymphomaniac and psychotic; she may be as defensive as he is and as full of confused drives and self-hatred, but she is also the Romantic in an unromantic land.

Works by Tennessee Williams

Cairo! Shanghai! Bombay! [with Bernice Dorothy Shapiro], 1935.

Headlines, 1936.

The Magic Tower, 1936.

Candles to the Sun, 1936.

Fugitive Kind, 1937.

Spring Storm, 1938.

Spring Song, 1938.

Battles of Angels 1940; also performed as *Orpheus Descending*, 1957.

The Long Goodbye, 1940.

This Property Is Condemned, 1942.

You Touched Me! [with Donald Windham], 1943.

The Gentleman Caller (screenplay), 1943.

The Glass Menagerie, 1944.

The Purification, 1944.

Stairs to the Roof, 1945.

Moony's Kid Don't Cry, 1946.

27 Wagons Full of Cotton, and Other One-Act Plays by Tennessee Williams, 1946.

The Last of My Solid Gold Watches, 1947.

Portrait of a Madonna, 1947.

A Streetcar Named Desire, 1947.

Lord Byron's Love Letter, 1947.

Auto-da-Fe, 1947.

Summer and Smoke 1947; also performed as *Eccentricities of a Nightingale*, 1964.

American Blues: Five Short Plays [first publication] (drama), 1948.

One Arm, and Other Stories, 1948.

The Rose Tattoo, 1950.

The Roman Spring of Mrs. Stone (novel), 1950.

Camino Real, 1953.

Hard Candy: A Book of Stories, 1954.

Cat on a Hot Tin Roof, 1955.

Something Unspoken, 1955.

Lord Byron's Love Letter (libretto), 1955.

The Case of the Crushed Petunias, 1957.

Sweet Bird of Youth, 1956.

In the Winter of Cities (poetry), 1956.

Baby Doll (screenplay), 1956.

Orpheus Descending: A Play in Three Acts, 1957.

Period of Adjustment, 1958.

Suddenly Last Summer, 1958.

Talk to Me Like the Rain and Let Me Listen, 1958.

I Rise in Flame, Cried the Phoenix, 1959.

The Night of the Iguana, 1959.

Three Players of a Summer Game, and Other Stories, 1960.

The Milk Train Doesn't Stop Here Anymore, 1962.

The Gnadiges Fraulein 1966; also performed as *The Latter Days of a Celebrated Soubrette*, 1974.

The Mutilated, 1966.

The Two-Character Play 1967; also performed as *Out Cry*, 1971.

Androgyne, Mon Amour (poetry), 1967.

The Knightly Quest: A Novella and Four Short Stories, 1966.

The Seven Descents of Myrtle 1968; also performed as *Kingdom of Earth*, 1975.

Dragon Country [first publication] (drama), 1969.

In the Bar of a Tokyo Hotel, 1969.

Confessional 1971; also performed as *Small Craft Warnings*, 1972.

I Can't Imagine Tomorrow, 1971.

The Theatre of Tennessee Williams. 7 vols., 1971.

Eight Mortal Ladies Possessed: A Book of Stories, 1974.

Moise and the World of Reason (novel), 1975.

Memoirs, 1975.

The Red Devil Battery Sign, 1976.

This Is (An Entertainment), 1976.

Vieux Carre, 1977.

Creve Coeur 1978; also performed as *A Lovely Sunday for Creve Coeur*, 1979.

Tiger Tail, 1978.

Where I Live: Selected Essays, 1978.

Clothes for a Summer Hotel, 1980.

Some Problems for the Moose Lodge, 1980; also performed as *A House Not Meant to Stand*, 1981.

Will Mr. Merriweather Return from Memphis?, 1980.

Something Cloudy, Something Clear, 1981.

The Bag People (novel), 1982.

It Happened the Day the Sun Rose, and Other Stories (short stories), 1982.

Collected Stories (short stories), 1985.

Annotated Bibliography

Bloom, Harold, ed. *Modern Critical Views: Tennessee Williams.* New York: Chelsea House Publications, 1987.

This collection contains views on multiple topics in Williams' scholarship. Of particular note for students of *Streetcar* are the essays by Alvin B. Kiernan, Gilbert Debusscher, and Joseph N. Riddell

Falk, Signi. *Tennessee Williams: Second Edition.* Boston: G.K. Hall & Co., 1978.

In this book length examination, Falk looks equally at the playwright's biography as well as major character archetypes within Williams's plays, stories and memoirs.

Griffin, Alice. *Understanding Tennessee Williams.* Columbia, South Carolina: University of South Carolina Press, 1995.

This book gives a general overview of Williams's most popular plays. Her coverage of *Streetcar* includes a useful scene by scene breakdown as well as thematic analysis.

Gross, Robert F., ed. *Tennessee Williams: A Casebook.* New York: Routledge, 2002.

This collection looks at a number of the plays through a variety of critical lenses. Frank Bradley's essay, "Two Transient Plays: *A Streetcar Named Desire* and *Camino Real*" is of particular note for *Streetcar* scholars as it compares the archetypal journeying characters in both plays.

Hurrell, John D. *Two Modern American Tragedies: Reviews and Criticism of Death of a Salesman and A Streetcar Named Desire.* New York: Charles Scribner's Sons, 1961.

Created as a research tool for students, this book contains essays on the nature of tragedy and the ways in which both plays fulfil the definition thereof, reviews and early criticism, commentary from the playwrights themselves and helpful appendices for research paper writing.

Jackson, Esther Merle. *The Broken World of Tennessee Williams*. Madison, Wisconsin: University of Wisconsin Press, 1965.

Jackson's study investigates structure, morality, and the cultural context in which and with which Williams wrote his plays.

Kolin, Philip C. ed., *Confronting Tennessee Williams's "A Streetcar Named Desire": Essays in Critical Pluralism*. Westport, CT: Greenwood Press, 1993.

This book collects some of the best recent criticism to focus on *Streetcar*, gathered by one of the leading Williams' scholars.

Martin, Robert A, ed. *Critical Essays on Tennessee Williams*. New York: G.K. Hall & Co., 1997.

This book collects both essays and reviews of the major Williams plays as well as essays which provide a more general overview of the writer's work.

Murphy, Brenda. *Tennessee Williams and Elia Kazan: A Collaboration in the Theatre*. Cambridge: Cambridge University Press, 1992.

This book provides useful insight into the collaborative process shared by Williams and Kazan. For scholars of *Streetcar*, Murphy takes special care to articulate the ways in which Kazan influenced the thematic focus of the play and some of its revisions.

O'Connor, Jacqueline. *Dramatizing Dementia: Madness in the Plays of Tennessee Williams*. Bowling Green, OH: Bowling Green University Popular Press, 1997.

O'Connor wrote a book length study examining the portrayal of madness within the plays. Her discussion of Blanche DuBois's descent into madness and Williams's balanced portrayal of the character are valuable.

Pagan, Nicholas. *Rethinking Literary Biography: A Postmodern Approach to Tennessee Williams*. Rutherford: Farleigh Dickinson University Press, 1993.

Pagan's study attempts to use Williams's life as a text with which to compare and interpret Williams's fictional work (plays, stories, etc). He suggests that the interplay between the autobiographical writings and his literary work suggests a broader understanding of both.

Roudane, Matthew C., ed. *The Cambridge Companion to Tennessee Williams.* Cambridge: Cambridge University Press, 1997.

A collection of critical essays by leading scholars. Of particular interest are essays by Felicia Hardison Londre, R. Barton Palmer and Gilbert Debusscher.

Stanton, Stephen S., ed. *Tennessee Williams: A Collection of Critical Essays.* Englewood Cliffs, NJ: Prentice Hall, Inc., 1977.

This collection includes essays by many important critics in Williams' scholarship, Ruby Cohn, Thomas P. Adler, Nancy Tischler and Esther Merle Jackson among them.

Tharpe, Jac, ed. *Tennessee Williams: A Tribute.* Jackson: University Press of Mississippi, 1977.

A comprehensive collection of containing essays on the major plays, Williams's life and position with the canon of American drama, his themes, techniques, poetry, prose and critical reception.

Thompson, Judith J. *Tennessee Williams' Plays: Memory, Myth, and Symbol.* New York: Peter Lang Publishing, 1987.

Thompson closely examines eight of the major plays, paying particular attention, as the title suggests to the use of myth, symbol and metaphor within the works.

Voss, Ralph F., ed. *Magical Muse: Millennial Essays on Tennessee Williams.* Tuscaloosa: University of Alabama Press, 2002.

A collection of essays from leading scholars including Nancy Tischler and Philip C. Kolin. Tischler examines the rape of Blanche and Kolin looks at the character of Mitch as an example of the typical ineffectual Williams' suitor.

Contributors

Harold Bloom is Sterling Professor of the Humanities at Yale University. He is the author of over 20 books, including *Shelley's Mythmaking* (1959), *The Visionary Company* (1961), *Blake's Apocalypse* (1963), *Yeats* (1970), *A Map of Misreading* (1975), *Kabbalah and Criticism* (1975), *Agon: Toward a Theory of Revisionism* (1982), *The American Religion* (1992), *The Western Canon* (1994), and *Omens of Millennium: The Gnosis of Angels, Dreams, and Resurrection* (1996). *The Anxiety of Influence* (1973) sets forth Professor Bloom's provocative theory of the literary relationships between the great writers and their predecessors. His most recent books include *Shakespeare: The Invention of the Human* (1998), a 1998 National Book Award finalist, *How to Read and Why* (2000), *Genius: A Mosaic of One Hundred Exemplary Creative Minds* (2002), *Hamlet: Poem Unlimited* (2003), and *Where Shall Wisdom be Found* (2004). In 1999, Professor Bloom received the prestigious American Academy of Arts and Letters Gold Medal for Criticism, and in 2002 he received the Catalonia International Prize.

Camille-Yvette Welsch is an instructor of writing at the Pennsylvania State University. Her work has appeared in *Calyx* and *Red Cedar Review*, and *Barrow Street*.

Normand Berlin is a professor emeritus of English at the University of Massachusetts, Amherst. He is the author of *The Secret Cause: A Discussion of Tragedy* and *The Base String: The Underworld in Elizabethan Drama* among others.

Frank Bradley is Associate Professor of theater and chair of the department of Performing and Visual Arts at American University of Cairo. He is also the artistic director of the Wallace Theatre.

Bert Cardullo is Professor of theatre and drama at the University of Michigan as well as the theater critic for The

Hudson Review. His numerous books include *Conversations with Stanley Kauffman, Vittoria De Sica: Director, Actor Screenwriter* and *What is Dramaturgy?* among others.

Ruby Cohn is a theatre scholar and Professor Emerita of Comparative Drama at University of California, Davis. She is the author or editor of many books, *The Comic Gamut, Samuel Beckett: A Collection of Criticism, Back to Beckett* and *A Beckett Canon*, among others.

Mary Ann Corrigan is the director of the Georgetown University Center for Professional Development, part of the graduate program in Communication, Culture, and Technology. She received a PhD in English from University of Michigan, and taught at Georgetown before returning to school to study computer programming.

Arthur Ganz has taught at the City College of the City University of New York. He is author of *Realms of the Self: Variations on a Theme in Modern Drama* and *George Bernard Shaw*, has edited *Harold Pinter: A Collection of Critical Essays*, and has written many more articles.

Alice Griffin is Professor Emerita and former director of graduate studies in English at Herbery H. Lehman College of the City University of New York. Her books include *Rebels and Lovers: Shakespeare's Young Heroes and Heroines, Understanding Tennessee Williams* and *Understanding Arthur Miller*.

Britton J. Harwood is a Professor of English at Miami University of Ohio. He is the author of *Piers Plowman and the Problem of Belief* and *Class and Gender in Early English Literature: Intersections* with Gillian R. Overing.

Esther Merle Jackson is Professor Emerita of Theatre and Drama at the University of Wisconsin at Madison. She is the author of *The Broken World of Tennessee Williams* among other scholarly publications.

Philip C. Kolin is a professor of English the University of Southern Mississippi, Hattiesburg. He is the author of more than twenty books ranging from Shakespeare to Tennessee Williams. His work includes *The Tennessee Williams Encyclopedia* and *Confronting Tennessee Williams's* A Streetcar Named Desire: *Essays in Critical Pluralism*, among others

Brenda Murphy is Professor of English at the University of Connecticut. She is the editor of *The Cambridge Companion to American Women Playwrights* and the author of *Tennessee Williams and Elia Kazan: A Collaboration in the Theatre*.

Jacqueline O'Connor is an Associate Professor of English at Boise State University. She is the author of *Dramatizing Dementia: Madness in the Plays of Tennessee Williams* as well as many scholarly articles.

Nicholas Pagan is a professor at Eastern Mediterranean University. He is the author of *Rethinking Literary Biography: A Postmodern Approach to Tennessee Williams*, among other titles.

Leonard Quirino is a Professor of English at Western Connecticut State College, Danbury. He is author of *Tennessee Williams' Persistent* Battle of Angels.

John M. Roderick is Chair and Professor of Hillyer English at the University of Hartford.

Nancy Tischler is Professor Emerita of English and Humanities at the Pennsylvania State University. She is the author of *Men and Women of the Bible: A Reader's Guide*, *Student Companion to Tennessee Williams* and editor of *The Selected Letters of Tennessee Williams, Volume I: 1920–1945*.

 Acknowledgments

"Complimentary in *A Streetcar Named Desire*" by Normand Berlin. From *Tennessee Williams: A Tribute*, Jac Thorpe, ed. Pp. 98–100. © 1977 University Press of Mississippi.

"Two Transient Plays: A Streetcar Named Desire and Camino Real" by Frank Bradley. From *Tennessee Williams: A Casebook*, Robert F. Gross, ed. Pp. 54–56.© 2002 by Routledge. Reproduced by permission of Routledge/Taylor & Francis Books Inc.

"Drama of Intimacy and Tragedy of Incomprehension" by Bert Cordullo. From *Tennessee Williams: A Tribute*, Jac Thorpe, ed. Pp. 140–143. © 1977 University Press of Mississippi.

"The Garrulous Grotesques of Tennessee Williams" by Ruby Cohn. From *Tennessee Williams: A Collection of Critical Essays*, Stephen S. Stanton, ed. Pp. 48–51. © 1971 by Indiana University Press.

"Realism and Theatricalism in A Streetcar Named Desire" by Mary Ann Corrigan. From *Critical Essays on Tennessee Williams*, Robert Martin, ed. Pp. 89–91. © 1997, G.K. Hall. Reprinted by permission of The Gale Group.

"Tennessee Williams: A Desperate Morality" by Arthur Ganz. From *Tennessee Williams: A Collection of Critical Essays*, Stephen S. Stanton, ed. Pp. 127–128. © 1977 by Arthur Ganz. Reprinted with permission of the author.

Understanding Tennessee Williams by Alice Griffin. Pp. 67–71. © 1995 by University of S. Carolina Press.

"Tragedy as Habit: A Streetcar Named Desire" by Britton J. Harwood. From *Tennessee Williams: A Tribute*. Jac Thorpe, ed. Pp. 110–112. © 1977 University Press of Mississippi.

"The Broken World of Tennessee Williams" by Esther Merle Jackson. Pp. 80–82. © 1965 The University of Wisconsin Press. Reprinted by permission of The University of Wisconsin Press.

Index